BEST "NEW" AFRICAN POETS 2025 ANTHOLOGY/ ANTHOLOGIE DES MEILLEURS "NOUVEAUX" POÈTES AFRICAINS 2025/ ANTOLOGIA DOS MELHORES "NOVOS" AFRICANOS 2025

Edited and Compiled by:
Tendai Rinos Mwanaka
Lorna Zita
Arnold Kobi Mondo

Mwanaka Media and Publishing Pvt Ltd,
Chitungwiza Zimbabwe
*
Creativity, Wisdom and Beauty

Publisher: *Mmap*
Mwanaka Media and Publishing Pvt Ltd
24 Svosve Road, Zengeza 1
Chitungwiza Zimbabwe
mwanaka@yahoo.com
mwanaka13@gmail.com
www.africanbookscollective.com/publishers/mwanaka-media-and-publishing
https://facebook.com/MwanakaMediaAndPublishing/

Distributed in and outside N. America by African Books Collective
orders@africanbookscollective.com
www.africanbookscollective.com

ISBN: 978-1-77928-531-7
EAN: 9781779285317

© Tendai Rinos Mwanaka 2025

All rights reserved.
No part of this book may be reproduced or transmitted in any form or by any means, mechanical or electronic, including photocopying and recording, or be stored in any information storage or retrieval system, without written permission from the publisher

DISCLAIMER
All views expressed in this publication are those of the author and do not necessarily reflect the views of *Mmap*.

About Editors

Tendai Rinos Mwanaka is a multidisciplinary artist, writer, musician, editor, publisher and producer with over 70 individual books and curated anthologies published in US, Northern Ireland, UK, Cameroon and Zimbabwe. He has 5 music albums, with new album, *For Mberikwazvo: The Winter After* (2025) recently released and his music is playing in at least 18 radio stations in US, Canada, UK, France, Israel, Brazil and Australia. He has hundreds of paintings and drawings, thousands of photographs, some exhibited, published and sold. His pieces have appeared in over 500 journals in over 35 countries and his books and writing is translated into at least 11 languages. You can find him here: https://m.facebook.com/tendai.mwanaka

Lorna Zita: É escritora, roteirista é autora de obra raízes e gritos que exploram temas como identidade, memória e resistência, É membro da Mwasa (National Writer Association of South Africa) e membro fundador do Círculo Académico de Letras e Artes de Moçambique. Representou Moçambique no festival BBC Contains Strong Language realizado no Reino.

Mondo Kobi Arnold est un poète, écrivain et scientifique congolais, né à Kinshasa, capitale de la République Démocratique du Congo. Il est diplômé en Latin et Philosophie, aussi Licencié en Relations internationales à l'Université de Kinshasa. Amoureux de la science et de la littérature et auteur de plusieurs poèmes et œuvres scientifiques. Sa passion dans la poésie date depuis son enfance. Sa poésie est marquée par une emphase sur l'humanisme, le vouloir vivre ensemble avec un accent particulier sur l'amour, la justice et la solidarité.

Table of Contents

untitled dub poem I: *Aryan Kaganof (South Africa)*
untitled dub poem II: *Aryan Kaganof*
untitled dub poem III: *Aryan Kaganof*
Grief Residues: *Victor Unachukwu (Nigeria)*
How Do You Spell Home: *Victor Unachukwu*
On grammar of Survival: *Victor Unachukwu*
An Awakening of Souls: *Okolo Chinua (Nigeria)*
As a Comma Gliding through torn Edifices: *Okolo Chinua*
A Declaration of Intention: *Okolo Chinua*
Always this internal struggle with loneliness: *Abigail George (South Africa)*
When you came into my life: *Abigail George*
To two female poets, one Israeli and another Palestinian, from a South African poetess: *Abigail George*
AFRICAN WOMAN: *Vihje ben Nkhunga (Malawi)*
When God Sat Beside Me It was a quiet revelation in the hush of dawn: *Athalia Pule (Botswana)*
Rock bottom: *Athalia Pule*
The heart pines: *Athalia Pule*
Shore of Eternity: *Muhammad Ghazali (Nigeria)*
Where My Heart Is?: *Muhammad Ghazali*
Nightmare: *Muhammad Ghazali*
Northern Africa Nations: *Ivan Gaćina (Croatia/South Africa)*
Whispers In The Night: *Abigail Vanessa Bwakila (Tanzania)*
Labyrinth: *Abigail Vanessa Bwakila*
Mirror This, Mirror That: *Abigail Vanessa Bwakila*
On Words Refusing to Die: *William Khalipwina Mpina (Malawi)*

Even After We're Gone: *William Khalipwina Mpina*
This Graveyard Called My Country: *William Khalipwina Mpina*
On a clear Day ....: *Lucas Zulu (South Africa)*
Bellum: *Lucas Zulu*
Sanctuary: *Lucas Zulu*
Home; *Bradley Nsukuzokuduma Moyo (Zimbabwe)*
In Between: *Bradley Nsukuzokuduma Moyo*
the fisherman: *Archie Swanson (South Africa)*
the inky black: *Archie Swanson*
punting the Cam: *Archie Swanson*
THE WIND KNOWS NOTHING: *Emman Usman Shehu (Nigeria)*
SHADOW'S PACE: *Emman Usman Shehu*
TALKING POINT: *Emman Usman Shehu*
Beauty on the road: *Oscar Gwiriri (Zimbabwe)*
The song: *Oscar Gwiriri*
Love: *Oscar Gwiriri*
Zenzele Ndebele: *Jabulani Mzinyathi (Zimbabwe)*
Desert: *Jabulani Mzinyathi*
Suits: *Adiela Akoo (South Africa)*
THE WORLD OUTSIDE MY WINDOW: *Adiela Akoo*
I WILL KEEP YOU, BROTHER!: *Ntensibe Joseph (Uganda)*
ODE TO THE PILGRIM (*To the Pilgrim that never came back*- THE LITTLE DRUMMER BOY): *Ntensibe Joseph*
I WILL SUMMON MY GHOSTS: *Ntensibe Joseph*
I'LL FLY AWAY: *Emmanuel Tumwesige (Uganda)*
WOLVES: *Abdullatif Khalid Eberhard (Uganda)*
TO LILITH: *Abdullatif Khalid Eberhard*
LONDON BRIDGE IS FALLING: *Orji Chidiebere (Nigeria)*

Lazybones: *Martin Chrispine Juwa (Malawi)*
Mother to Daughter: *Martin Chrispine Juwa*
Night Dancers; *Martin Chrispine Juwa*
story of a dog: *Anton Krueger (South Africa)*
how foil absorbs blood: *Richeal Barnes (Ghana)*
back seat girls: *Richeal Barnes*
WALKING ON THE RIM OF RAIN: *Abubakar A. Yunusa (Nigeria)*
THE MAP THAT BURNS: *Abubakar A. Yunusa*
TO THE CHILD WHO HID BEHIND TOMORROW: *Abubakar A. Yunusa*
Le mien: *Nellah Nonkondlo Mtanenhlabathi (Zimbabwe)*
You just go to HELL!: *Nellah Nonkondlo Mtanenhlabathi*
Dancing with the Devil: *Nellah Nonkondlo Mtanenhlabathi*
Burning Soil: *Innocent Chima Ogoke (Nigeria)*
Tongues of Reconciliation: *Innocent Chima Ogoke*
PEACE: *Ibadin Kingsley (Nigeria)*
VILLAGE BOY: *Agufa Kivuya (Kenya)*
WHERES THE KING: *Agufa Kivuya*
IN THE RACE; *Agufa Kivuya*
DREAMSIDE EXCHANGE: *Francis Otole (Nigeria)*
CANONS FOR CANNONS: *Francis Otole*
TOWARDS PERFECTION: *Francis Otole*
The Noon: *Imemba Emmanuel Ikechukwu (Nigeria)*
Do not label me a murderer of trees: *Imemba Emmanuel Ikechukwu*
Let them eat what they serve others: *Obinna Chilekezi (Nigeria)*
BULLETIN BUGS: *Ekundayo Asifat (Nigeria)*
IYA GBOGBO (My step mother): *Ekundayo Asifat*

This is Our Homeland Too: *Tlotlisang David Mhlambiso (South Africa)*
Exile me!: *Tlotlisang David Mhlambiso*
If I Make It Back Home: *Tlotlisang David Mhlambiso*
Fresh Tears: *Wafula Khisa (Kenya)*
Reign of Terror: *Wafula Khisa*
You're Not the Friend I Knew: *Wafula Khisa*
HER LOST LOVER: *Ngcali Angelica Xhegwana (South Africa)*
The Wilderness: *Janet Patricia Chikoja (Malawi)*
Zomba Mountain: *Janet Patricia Chikoja*
CAUTION: *Janet Patricia Chikoja*
Waiting for the Sun: *Yvonnie S. Kunkeyani (Just Sam) (Malawi)*
Of old habits that die hard: *Yvonnie S. Kunkeyani (Just Sam)*
Her Nine Lives: *Yvonnie S. Kunkeyani (Just Sam)*
The Museum: *Kirsten Miller (South Africa)*
Building walls: *Kirsten Miller*
Ask the Sea: *Kirsten Miller*
KING MAKERS: *Lungisile Goodwell Mselana (South Africa)*
SCRUPULOUS CAVES: *Lungisile Goodwell Mselana*
RELENTLESS DEMONS: *Lungisile Goodwell Mselana*
Makanai's Rest: *Ewurama Tawiah Welbeck (Ghana)*
The Sound of Rain: *Ewurama Tawiah Welbeck*
The Return of Peace: *Ewurama Tawiah Welbeck*
GLOBAL HARMONY: *Maryam Shitu Abdulkadir (Nigeria)*
RECIPROCRITY: *Maryam Shitu Abdulkadir*
ART-AURAL: *Maryam Shitu Abdulkadir*
SILENT CRY: *Comfort Adjeiwaa (Ghana)*
MASKED: *Comfort Adjeiwaa*
WHISPERS OF ECHOES: *Comfort Adjeiwaa*

WHEN BOYI WAS ASKED TO DEFINE LOVE...: *Alfred Inkah Kamwendo (Malawi)*
Dear ABITI MULI: *Alfred Inkah Kamwendo*
IN MEMORIAM: *Alfred Inkah Kamwendo*
Allegories: *Ismail Bala (Nigeria)*
Offering: *Ismail Bala*
And Then Now: *Ismail Bala*
DOWNTOWN HARARE: *Simbarashe Nyatsanza (Zimbabwe)*
THE CONFIRMATION OF ROT: *Simbarashe Nyatsanza*
POETS DON'T GET PAID HERE: *Simbarashe Nyatsanza*
LEFT HUNG OUT TO DRY: *Mathews Mhango (Malawi)*
SILENT SCARS: *Mathews Mhango*
TWO SHOTS OF PAIN: *Mathews Mhango*
DRUM OF PEACE: *Ophoke Leonard Onyebuchi (Nigeria)*
Waning Crown, Mother Land!: *Ophoke Leonard Onyebuchi*
Uniting Africa's Children: *Ophoke Leonard Onyebuchi*
POETICS OF THE POETS: *Usman Danjuma Osu (Nigeria)*
WHO LOVES THE MATCH?: *Usman Danjuma Osu*
SHOULD WE FORGIVE VEGETABLE LOVE?: *Usman Danjuma Osu*
STAR, PERSONIFIED: *Bucknor Esther (Nigeria)*
FAR ENOUGH FOR TWO: *Bucknor Esther*
FRAGMENTS THAT SELFLESSLY FORGE YOU: *Bucknor Esther*
SOMETIME IN JUNE: *Denis Waswa Barasa*
The Rain Came: *Denis Waswa Barasa*
The Bat: *Denis Waswa Barasa*
Existence in the Vacuum: *Susan Gamuchirai Muchirahondo (Zimbabwe)*

Affinity: *Susan Gamuchirai Muchirahondo*
War cry: *Tanatswa Nyamayaro (Zimbabwe)*
Almost Christmas: *Tanatswa Nyamayaro*
The Mirror Lied: *Ifechieme Chima-Ogoke (Nigeria)*
The Child I Used to Be: *Ifechieme Chima-Ogoke*
The Voice I Found: *Ifechieme Chima-Ogoke*
The warrior of Likoma: *Immulanie Makande (Malawi)*
Bury me where: *David Chasumba (Zimbabwe)*
You make me laugh: *David Chasumba*
Sowing in Tears: *David Chasumba*
BABYLON: *Sithembele Xhegwana (SouthAfrica)*
VOICES IN THE WIND: *Sithembele Xhegwana*
The prize: *Justice Masangano(Malawi)*
River rock: *Justice Masangano*
The belly of the beast: *Justice Masangano*
Looking Straight Into My Eyes: *Moore Ngwenya (Kingdom of Eswatini)*
Rumblings: *Raphael Onyejizu (Nigeria)*
Sahara Run: *Raphael Onyejizu*
Wonders!: Raphael Onyejizu
THE HEART IS A WILD ANIMAL: *Paul Oluwafemi David (Nigeria)*
We love South Africa: *Deena Padayachee (South Africa)*
Passez-moi des mots: *Adamou Idé (Niger)*
Les dictateurs: *Adamou Idé (Niger)*
Poète, reviens: *Adamou Idé (Niger)*
L'idéal: *Dan Mbo Kuba (République Démocratique du Congo)*
Qui s'éveille: *Dan Mbo Kuba (République Démocratique du Congo)*
Le chemin du partage: *Dan Mbo Kuba (République Démocratique du Congo)*

La maîtresse de Dieu: *Fraubi Amel*
Hier encore (Enfants de la rue): *Fraubi Amel*
À toi qui part: *Fraubi Amel*
Son de sirène: *Kane Nabalemwendé Athanase (Burkina Faso)*
Siège: *Kane Nabalemwendé Athanase (Burkina Faso)*
Laissés-pour-compte: *Kane Nabalemwendé Athanase (Burkina Faso)*
Le Destin: *Mondo Kobi Arnold (République Démocratique du Congo)*
Nouvelle journée: *Mondo Kobi Arnold (République Démocratique du Congo)*
Extase: *Mondo Kobi Arnold (République Démocratique du Congo)*
À jamais ma langue ne se vêtira de crainte: *Wankpo Franck*
Intellectuel: *Wankpo Franck*
Chair odieuse: *Wankpo Franck*
Impotentes sem Deus: *Maria Menezes*
Ergue-te: *Maria Menezes*
Um menino na praia: *Maria Menezes*
Inferno: *Orlando Mussaengana*
Contra *sensu*: *Orlando Mussaengana*
As 3 faces da moeda: *Orlando Mussaengana*
I Quiçá Amor: *Jéssica Samara*
II Quiçá Amor: *Jéssica Samara*
III Quiçá Amor: *Jéssica Samara*
Fragmentos do acaso: *Gerson Leonardo Matusse*
A Técnica da Coisa: *Gerson Leonardo Matusse*
A Fénix; *Lorna Zita*
Amores vêm e vão: *Lorna Zita*
Àfrica e o dilema da fé; *Jaime Fernando Sigaúque*
Cobra Versus Maria Café: *Jaime Fernando Sigaúque*
Piratas das caraíbas: *Jaime Fernando Sigaúque*

Contributors' Bio Notes

Aryan Kaganof is publisher and editor of the South African cultural journal herri (https://herri.org.za/10/).

A Nigerian, **Victor Unachukwu** is a writer and poet who demonstrates a fervent commitment to addressing social issues through his work. By giving voice to the challenges faced by society, he seeks to spark meaningful change. He holds an MA in English and Literature, and currently an MFA candidate at the University of Kentucky. His poems have been published in Adelaide magazine, DLit 'Review, and Spill word press.

Okolo Chinua is a writer who writes for many reasons, the beauty of tomorrow being the foremost. Currently, he lives and writes from the suburbs of Onitsha, Anambra State, Nigeria.

Abigail George is a South African poet. Her poems have been translated into Italian. She is also a journalist and book reviewer. Her latest book is Songs For Palestine: Struggle Poems. She has written three novels. Her work has most recently appeared in Critical Muslim's Water issue.

Vihje ben Nkhunga - an avid reader, writer and ardent poet. A member of Malawi Writers Union (MAWU), Poetry Association of Malawi (PAM) and PEN international (Malawi Chapter). Published in anthologies and local newspapers. Ghost written several prose and poetry works. Edited several short stories that won local prizes, edited Tiseke and the Tree(a children's book by Aubrey Chinguwo). Established Writer's Club at Nanthomba Community Day Secondary school. A practicing medical practitioner, but a great literally enthusiast

Athalia Pule is a budding wordsmith, weaving tapestries of verse that explore the intersections of spirituality, faith, pain, and social justice. With a voice that resonates with authenticity and vulnerability, she crafts poetry that inspires, uplifts, and sparks meaningful conversations. As a testament to the transformative power of art, Athalia's writing has been a sanctuary, offering solace and strength in the face of life's complexities. Through her work, she aims to kindle empathy, foster connection, and illuminate the human experience.

Muhammad Ghazali is a native of Kano State, Nigeria. He has Bachelors and Masters Degrees from Bayero University, Kano. He has been teaching English Language and Literature since 2006 and presently at Kano Capital School. Aside from taking English Weekend classes at Aminci Radio English, he also teaches at numerous colleges and polytechnic, and nominated for literacy programmes by Kano State Senior Secondary Schools Management Board. He also voluntarily teaches and conduct personal lessons on English and Literature as part of his social responsibility. More than two hundred poems were written and some of which are published in his name. Similarly, he is a member of Junior Chamber International (JCI), where he served as President 2022 for JCI Kano, and attendended conferences and conventions. Furthermore, he is an Assistant Consultant at Sumar Consultancy Network. He is polite, kind and humble, and has good upbringing from his noble parents. He is now blessed with two children. Thank you

My name is **Abigail Vanessa Bwakila**. I am a twenty-nine year old Tanzanian poetess who has been writing poems from the tender age of nine. I have a compilation of a hundred poems called A peek into my wayward mind that is currently in the process of publication. I am working on the next hundred poems to publish day by day. I write about a myriad of things, such as; depression, my life, and the way my mind works, just to name a few. I attained a degree in Animal Science and I am an Animal Scientist by profession.

William Khalipwina Mpina is an economist and data analyst at the Malawi Revenue Authority, where he utilizes data to influence policy and strategy. Beyond his work with numbers, he is a celebrated literary figure—serving as a poet, editor, and advocate for storytelling. He co-edited Walking the Battlefield (2020), a bilingual poetry anthology focused on Covid-19, and authored Mooning the Morning (2022, Montfort Media), a collection that explores themes of introspection and rebellion. His children's book, Kamwala Kodabwitsa (2024), which is part of PEN International's Invisible Child Project, highlights his commitment to fostering young imaginations. Additionally, he recently published a collection of short stories titled Stranger in Her Own Skin (2025) in Zimbabwe, now available at https://www.africanbookscollective.com/books/stranger-in-her-own-skin. Mpina's influence extends throughout the literary community. He served as a judge for the 2024 IHRAM SADC Literary Prize in Poetry, is the Treasurer General of the Malawi Union of Academic and Nonfiction Authors, and is an Executive Committee member of PEN Malawi. At the intersection of economics, literature, and advocacy, he is crafting a legacy that reflects both analytical rigour and lyrical creativity—leaving a significant mark on Malawi's cultural landscape.

Lucas Zulu lives in South Africa, eMalahleni, Kwaguqa, Mpumalanga Province. His works is published widely in Zimbabwe, Nigeria, Botswana and North America.

Bradley Nsukuzokuduma Moyo is a Zimbabwe page poet and author. Moyo is a Bulawayo based poet and his work explores a plethora of themes but largely his poetry is more of social commentary. He seeks to create a platform for African conscious conversations, to share the modern African narrative and to give a voice to his generation. In 2024 Bradley became the pioneer of The Aries Rage Mentorship program which led to his first publication; Thalitha Koumi. In the same year Dream Discovery Publishers awarded him the second runner up award in the poetry career at the Annual Book Awards which were held in Gweru by Dream Discovery Publishers. He has been featured on various platforms such The Mud Journal, The Standard and many others.

Archie Swanson has published six collections of poetry – *the stretching of my sky* (2018), *the shores of years* (2019), *beyond a distant edge* (2021), *of clay* (2022), *at the estuary* (2024), and *winnowings* (2025). He is widely anthologised and awarded, and as librettist has collaborated extensively with composer Grant McLachlan. www.instagram.com/poetarchie

Emman Usman Shehu hails from Maradun, Zamfara State of Nigeria. He currently resides in Abuja, Nigeria's capital, where he works with the International Institute of Journalism. He is also involved with the Abuja Writers Forum (AWF), and is the editor of the literary journals - Cavalcade and Dugwe. Passionate about facilitating writing workshops, his poems have appeared in several print and online publications, including Okike, Kakaki ,Sentinel Poetry, PoetryWales, Stone Throw, Panoply and Best New African

Poets Anthology He has published four poetry collections: Questions For Big Brother, Open Sesame, Icarus Rising and The River Never Returns

Oscar Gwiriri is a Zimbabwean published in more than 70 books, both fiction and text books. His two books *Hatiponi* and *Chitima nditakure* were NAMA awards nominees in 2019. He is a Certified Forensic Investigations Professional (CFIP) and a Certified Information Systems Security Professional (CISSP). He also holds a *Master of Science in Strategic Management Degree, Bachelor of Business Administration, Associates of Arts in Business Administration, Diploma in Logistics and Transport (CILT, UK), Diploma in Workplace Safety and Health, Commanding United Nations Peacekeeping Operations Certificate*, and many other professional qualifications. He likes writing in his vernacular language (Shona) most.

Jabulani Mzinyathi is a free verse protest poet. Equal rights and justice is what he fights for. His poetry collections: Under The Steel Yoke , Righteous Indignation , In The Steel Talons, Among The Way , In The Inferno and The Stench are all scathing attacks against the "shitstem" that leaves the majority wallowing in abject poverty. Jabulani is also a budding novelist with a published chiShona novel entitled ' *Mumambure'*. Jabulani belongs to what he calls the Zimbolicious and BNAP stables. Jabulani is a former teacher, former magistrate now a lawyer in private practice. He loves roots, rock, reggae- which music shapes his life's perspective.

Adiela Akoo is an award-winning South African Poet. Her work has been published across the globe in English and in translation. She is the founding editor of the Quilled Ink Review biennial literary journal and founder of Quilled Ink Press. You may find out more about Adiela and her books here: https://linktr.ee/Adiela.Akoo

Ntensibe Joseph: Is passionate when it comes to writing poetry although he embraces other genres. Being a high school teacher of Literature and English, he works with young people with writing. He is also an editor. He graduated from Makerere University with honours in English and Literature. He is published in print and online. He appears in *Best New African Poets Anthology*, *Africanization and Americanization Anthology*, *when we Heard the Echoes* among others.

Emmanuel Tumwesige is a Ugandan educator at the secondary level whose writing started with the love for recreation of stories in words about social issues happening around. A poet whose (some) poems have been published in Africa in the BNAP series, South African 'Ode to Love' and Ugandan annual magazine on the UN Sustainable Development Goals- Kirabo Writes Magazine, and some given out for performances and presentations in gatherings and Music, Dance and Drama festivities.

Abdullatif Khalid Eberhard (The Sacred Poet) is Ugandan literary powerhouse, award-winning poet, educator (English, Literature), writer, word crosser, scriptwriter, essayist, content creator, storyteller, orator, mentor, public speaker, gender-based violence activist, hip-hop rapper, creative coach, editor, and spoken word artist who has experienced death more than a hundred times. He is the author of *Confessions of a Sinner vol. I*, *A Session in Therapy*, and *Confessions of a Sinner vol. II*. He offers creative writing services and performs at projects focused on brand/ campaign awareness, luncheons, corporate dinners, date nights, product launches, advocacy events, and concerts.

Orji Chidiebere was born on 20th January, 1986 to Sir, Gabriel Amadioha Orji and Mrs. Grace Waliezi Orji. He hails from Egbeda Town, Emohua Local Government Area of Rivers State. He had his Nursery and Primary School education at Risonpalm Staff Nur/Primary School, Elele-Estate and proceeded to Government Army Secondary School, Elele, for his secondary education. He holds a B.A. degree in English/Literary Studies which he got from University of Port Harcourt, Rivers State. He is currently running a Masters Programme at Ignatuies Ajuru University of Education, Rumuolumeni, Port Harcourt. His specialty is on research, gender studies, African-American-Caribbean Studies, Niger Delta literature, Oral Literature and Creative Writing.

Martin Chrispine Juwa is a History teacher from Lilongwe; Malawi. His work appears in numerous international anthologies, magazines and journals, including The Poet Magazine, Griots of Ubuntu, JAYL Vol. 2, 4 BNAP anthologies, Held magazine, 3 Mental Health anthologies, Orchards Journal, Southern Humanities Review, Afreecan Magazine, Strange Births, Pangolin Review, Libero America Journal, and Pensive Journalof Spirituality. He has a debut poetry anthology titled *Drifting Smoke* (Scribble Publications, Malawi, 2020).

More recently, **Anton Krueger** has been experimenting with spoken word collaborations – some improvised, some not – with musicians including Tony Bental, Warrick Sony, Zanethemba Midyogolo, Geoff Tracey, Francois le Roux (the HA! man) and jazz legend Paul Hanmer. Otherwise, he's written plays, memoir, short stories, criticism, arts journalism and a manifesto on Amateurism. Sample his work here: https://amateurist.weebly.com/writings.html.

Richeal Barnes is a Ghanaian Poet and a practicing-nurse at the Ankaful Nurse's Training College in Cape Coast. She loves reading and listening to history. She plays tennis during her leisure time. Barnes uses her poems to reexamine history, explore feminism, identity and self-discovery via her life experiences by making an attempt to bridge the gap between language and form. Her poem have appeared in The Journal of African Youth Literature, Spill Words Press, Nenta Journal African Global Network and the maiden edition of the Ghana Poetry Festival Anthology "What they say does have an end".

Abubakar A. Yunusa is a Nigerian poet, essayist, and storyteller from Azare, Bauchi State. His works explore identity, memory, and resilience, and have appeared in various platforms across Africa. He is a multiple award-winning performance poet and essayist who draws inspiration from his community's struggles and dreams

Innocent Chima Ogoke is a Nigerian literary scholar, creative writer, and doctoral candidate in the Department of English at the University of Ibadan, specialising in African literature. His research interests encompass queer studies, trauma theory, decoloniality, and literature and new media. Ogoke has published scholarly articles in journals such as *Akshara* and *Ars Artium*, exploring themes of identity, sexuality, and postcolonial narratives. His creative works include the novella *Dark Prize*. He is affiliated with the Association of Nigerian Authors and the Society of Young Nigerian Writers, and has held leadership roles in literary organisations

Ibadin Kingsley is a poet known for his work, featured in the Abuja writers forum on Facebook. He is also associated with the people's poetry parliament. His work often explores themes of social and political issues, including the struggles of youth, corruption and the impact of political decisions on every day's life. He has won the Medal of Honour Award from Poetic Gladiators, Star Poet of the Week from African Poetry Giant and Certificate of Publishing from Modern Poetry Society, 2025. He is currently a lecturer in the English Department of Federal Capital Territory College of Education, Zuba, Abuja, Nigeria.

I am **Agufa Kivuya,** a poet, writer and yet to be published Author from Kenya. Been writing poem for over 10 years now

Francis Otole is a poet and author. His works have appeared in local and international magazines, journals, and anthologies. His debut collection of poems, Heaven is a Place on Earth made the shortlist of ANA- Association of Nigerian Authors poetry prize, 2024. He loves reading and writing. His marriage to his lovely wife is blessed with a set of twins.

Imemba Emmanuel Ikechukwu is a writer from Abia State, Nigeria. He has been long listed for the Blessing Kolajo poetry prize, 2024. His works have appeared in Teambooktu and Brittle Paper.

Ekundayo Asifat hails from Iwo, Osun State, Nigeria. A man of many parts, Mr. Asifat is a poet, orator, playwright, actor and Dancer. He had worked and retired as a School principal. He has, since retirement, been shuttling between Osun and Oyo States. Living an artistic life. His poems had been published in the defunct The Nigerian Review magazine, the defunct Third Eye newspaper, The Best new Africa Poets an Anthology, and Association of Nigerian Authors (Oyo State Chapter) publications.

Tlotlisang David Mhlambiso is a Masters Candidate in Languages in Education at the University of the Free State, Faculty of Education, Department of Languages in Education, from South Africa. He is a published author of three indigenous poetry books titled "Ukuphuma Kwelanga", "Phind' ubhale" and "Zizinto Zobomi" and a multilingual collection of short stories in IsiXhosa and English, "A Journey Worth the Ride". He has been named amongst the Mail and Guardian 200 Young South Africans 2025, JCI SA Top 20 2024, Sunday World Unsung Hero 2024, 100 SA Shining Stars 2023 and NYDA Education Sector Trailblazer 2023 and UFS EDSA Student of the Year 2023, for his contribution to the African narrative and other projects

Wafula Khisa is a Kenyan poet, writer and teacher. He has authored four books: *A Cock's Seduction Song & Poems (2019), When I Hear My Mother's Voice & Other Poems (2022), Beyond the Pulpit & Other Stories (2024) and Nearly Every Man is Mad? & Other Stories (2022)*. His work was long-listed for the Babishai Niwe Poetry Prize in 2018. His poetry and prose have appeared in various online literary journals and magazines and in print such as Nthanda Review, Writers Space Africa, The African Writer Magazine, Scarlet Leaf Review, Agape Review, The Elixir Magazine, The Antarctica Journal, Nalubaale Literary Review, Better Than Starbucks Poetry & Literary Magazine, The Armageddon and Other Stories, A Tale to Tell and the Best "New African poets Anthology series among others.

Ngcali Angelica Xhegwana was born on the 25th of November 2007 at St Dominics Private Hospital in East London. She is presently doing her Grade 12 at Byletts High School at Mooiplas, East London. Her first book, *Woodland* was published by Unicorn Press in 2018. Her second book, <u>Udyakalash'onkone</u> was published through the Via Afrika WPR program in 2019. Under the auspices of the National Research Foundation Intellectualisation of African Languages Chairmanship and Via Afrika, her book was one of the twelve titles that was identified that year. *Land Of Thorns*, a book in which she has collaborated with her father, is her third book. During 2020 she was one of the commissioned poets towards the 2020 AVBOB poetry anthology, *I Wish I Had Said... Vol. 4*.

Janet Patricia Chikoja is currently a full-time doctoral student in Humanities at Rhodes University (Republic of South Africa), Janet Chikoja is a lecturer in Business Communication at the Malawi University of Business and Applied Sciences (Malawi). Janet turns 42 years on 15th September 2023. She has published poems and short stories in Malawi National Newspapers. Her research interests are literature and the environment, representation of masculinity and gender-based violence, trauma literature, language and gender, sociolinguistics, and critical discourse analysis.

Yvonnie S. Kunkeyani is a content and creative writer from Malawi whose feature articles are published on an online bi-weekly magazine. She is a poet under the name JustSam who mostly writes page poetry but has a few for the stage which she has performed. A few of her poems have appeared online, but the most notable is Alice's Words which was published on Sheevolves Website.

Kirsten Miller is the author of novels, poems, short stories and non-fiction, and her work has been short-listed for a number of literary awards. She was twice the recipient of the Aziz

Hassim/Minara literary award and her novel *The Hum of the Sun* won the international Wilbur and Niso Smith Literature Award for best unpublished manuscript. The published novel was longlisted for the Dublin Literary Award, and the book was later translated into German. She holds an MA in writing and representation, and currently teaches language, writing and creativity at her studio in Durban, South Africa.

Lungisile Goodwell Mselana was born on the 14th of February 1973 around King William's town. So far, he has published two books, both in isiXhosa. The first is a collection of poems, *Izenjana*, published by Calabash Publishing Ltd. The second book is a collection of short stories, *Yaqhekek'ingqayi*, published through a generous grant from the South African Department of Sports, Recreation, Arts & Culture

Ewurama Tawiah Welbeck is a Ghanaian Creative writer and English Language teacher who uses poetry and prose to explore beauty, longing, intimacy, loss, love and memory. She finds existential meaning through amusement, tragedy, human experiences and strength. An alumnus of the SprinNG Writing Fellowship, some of her works appear in Writer's Space Africa, ArtisansQuill and Penned in Rage Literary Journal.

Maryam Shitu Abdulkadir is a female African poet from Nigeria (Kano state). She embarked on her journey of writing at the age of fourteen and is a store keeper of more than forty five poems and quotes. She is a passionate patriot that believes in the revivification of the African Heritage which stands out on its exclusively unique structure. Even though not acknowledged, Maryam trusts the might of pen over the sword in advocating for change in the light of global peace and prosperity. A quote of hers constitutes "if we must take to arms, then it should be with the pen and the voice"

My name is **Comfort Adjeiwaa**, a second year Communication Studies student at the University of Cape Coast, Ghana. I am 19 years of age. I am passionate about expressing myself through writing of poems and stories and also singing. With a keen interest in communication, I am excited to explore the world of ideas and creativity. When I am not studying, you can find me jamming to my favorite tunes or crafting stories. I am always looking to connect with like-minded individuals and learn from their experiences. The three poems below are titled; Silent cry, Masked, and lastly Whispers of echoes.

Alfred Inkah Kamwendo is a Malawian poet, playwright, director and actor among so many faces he wears. Kamwendo is a former president of the University of Malawi Writers Workshop in which he was a regular contributor. He has read his poems at Zomba City Festival, Easter Theatre Festival and many other presitigeous events. Alfred ia a holder of BA Humanities majoring in Literature in French and Theatre Studies from the University of Malawi.

Ismail Bala writes in English and Hausa. His poetry and translations have appeared in the UK, the USA, Canada, India and South Africa, in journals such as *Poetry Review*, *Ambit*, *New Coin*, *Ake Review*, *Lunaris, A Review of International English Literature* and *Aura Literary Arts Review*, among many others. Born and educated to university level in Kano, he did his post-graduate studies at Oxford. His poems have been translated into Latvian, Belarusian, Nepalese, Slovenian and Polish. He is a Fellow of the International Writing Programme of the University of Iowa. He is the author of *Line of Sight* (Praxis, 2020), *A Span of Something* (INKspired, 2024) and *Ivory Night* (KSR, 2024).

Simbarashe Nyatsanza is a Zimbabwean poet, writer, journalist and biotechnologist whose interdisciplinary career spans literature, journalism, and scientific research. His professional background includes work in Editorial Journalism, Education, Agricultural Research and Mining Engineering. Nyatsanza's literary work has been published in *Vernac News, Herri, Medium, and The Philosopher,* where he engages with themes of language, African identity, emotional resilience, and postcolonial critique. He also writes short fiction — one of his stories was adapted into a short film. His writing reflects analytical precision and lyrical depth, offering a nuanced perspective shaped by both scientific inquiry and literary tradition.

Mathews Mhango is an Internal Auditor by profession working in the public sector in Malawi. He likes to write poetry on different issues that affect society. He reads and writes poetry on a wide range of topics with tremendous passion. His poems have appeared on worldwide websites including *the poet Magazine* and in *Weekend Times Newspaper.*

Ophoke Leonard Onyebuchi is a dedicated advocate for international affairs and diplomacy, embodying a leadership style rooted in service. As an accomplished Administrator, Research and Data Analyst, and Negotiator, he also serves as a Mentor and is an active member of the International Studies Association (ISA). In 2021, he was honored as a prize winner in the Open Doors Olympiad in Politics and International Studies. Adventurous and solution-oriented, he approaches every task with a commitment to excellence. This dedication is reflected in his scholarly writings and engagements. Reading and writing are his lifelong passions, pursuits he will never abandon.

Mr Usman Danjuma Osu is a poet of Nasarawa state origin, Nigeria, West Africa; a Senior Lecturer teaching English Language, Literature and Creative writing; this he has done in many institutions of learning, and now in the Federal Polytechnic Nasarawa, Nasarawa State, Nigeria.

Bucknor Esther loves reading, music and writing poetry. She currently studies accounting at the university of Benin, Edo State.

Denis Waswa Barasa teaches English and Literature at The Immaculate Heart of Mary Luuya Girls High School in Bungoma County. He is passionate about drama, poetry, film and cultural studies. He has previously contributed to *Best New African Poets*.

Susan Gamuchirai Muchirahondo is a young Zimbabwean writer. She has been published in the Best New African Poets Anthology for 2018, 2019 and 2021 and 2022. She has also been published in the Zimbolicious Anthology. She mainly writes about abstract concepts, tragic romances, mental health issues and is a novelist and children's book author. She has been writing for over 10 years.

Tanatswa Nyamayaro is a young man of twenty-four years who stays in Harare, Zimbabwe. Currently, he is enrolled at Trust Academy where he is studying Marketing. Apart from learning, he is an avid writer with a penchant for poetry and has since co-published an anthology titled Tears of the Son. When not writing or studying, soccer is his escape.

Ifechieme Chima-Ogoke is a young Nigerian poet and emerging writer whose work explores themes of identity, resilience, and the lived realities of women and young people in Africa. She is currently an undergraduate student of English Language and Literature, where she combines her academic pursuit with a growing commitment to creative expression. Though still at the beginning of her literary journey, she is passionate about poetry as a space of healing, reflection, and advocacy. She hopes to use her writing to amplify silenced voices and to contribute to the expanding body of contemporary African poetry.

Immulanie Makande is an author, poet, and educator. His textbook *Integrated English for Senior Secondary* published by Acin, was approved for use in the Malawi's secondary curriculum. He also published two children stories. One of his poems; *Ndaipa*, was published in PEN Malawi's anthology titled *The Death of an Idea* and one of his short stories; *In the System* was published in the *Nation on Sunday*. Another short story *The Wade* was awarded a book prize by the MAWU/FMB Short Story Award. Immulanie has read his poetry in various spaces including at the International Conference on Oral Literature at Mzuzu University.

David Chasumba (snr) is a Zimbabwean Writer and Poet. He has published two short story collections with Carnelian Heart Publishing: 2023 NAMA award winning, *The Mad Man on First Street and Other Short Stories (2022)* and *Behind the Façade and Other Stories (2024)*. David's poems have been published by Kalahari Review, Ipikai Poetry Journal, British Haiku Society anthology (2023), in *Best "New" African Poets (2023)* anthology and in *MEN: An International Anthology of African and Latin American Writers, Volume 3* and in *Zimbolicious 9 anthology*. David lives in Bexhill-on-Sea, East Sussex, UK.

Dr Deena Padayachee is a medical doctor who is a winner of the Olive Schreiner and Nadine Gordimer prizes for his prose. He served as a columnist for the Sunday Times newspaper for many years. The doctor was a prescribed author for the matrics of Kwa Zulu Natal. Some of his writing has been translated into isiZulu, Xhosa, Tamil, Hindi and Italian. His poems have been published in South Africa, the USA, the UK, Australia, and India. His short stories have been anthologised widely including the university of Cambridge, Penguin, Readers' Digest's Best South African short stories, and in Chapman's A Century of South African short stories. He has been invited to speak about his prose by the universities of Tuebingen in Germany and Copenhagen in Denmark, the state university of Louisiana, the Teachers' college of Mauritius and the university of Zululand.

Paul Oluwafemi David is a Nigerian born Scientist, philosopher, poet and Apostle. He's the author of Beautiful Things Flower In The Rain selected for its original manuscript by a New York Press and Status Is Everything published in Nigeria. He's works have been published in Afrikana, African Writer, Bangalore Review, Kalahari Review, Tuck magazine, Pride magazine, Pride magazine, Artvilla,praxis magazine,the Muse,Three Drops From A Cauldron, Okadabooks,project Muse,Wrr and CWP.

H.R.H. H.E. Pangeran Prince Love YM Dato Rdo. Sri Academician Amb. Prof. Dr. Kt Exp. GM LM Genius **Ivan Gaćina** was born on April 15, 1981 in Zadar, the Republic of Croatia. His father was born in the Republic of South Africa, which connects him directly to the African diaspora. Ivan writes poetry (including haiku), short stories, aphorisms, and book reviews. He is a member of many associations and societies. His work has been translated into several foreign languages, and he has received more than 200 awards at literary competitions, in his country and abroad.

Adamou Idé est né à Niamey (Niger) le 22 novembre 1951. Il a fait ses études supérieures en droit à la Sorbonne (Université de Paris 1). Ancien Elève de l'Institut International d'Administration Publique de Paris, il écrit aussi bien en français que dans sa langue maternelle : le Songhay-Zarma. Sa production littéraire est variée (poésie, roman, nouvelle, essai) et porte essentiellement sur les drames humains (sécheresse, famine, violences contre les femmes), la lutte des peuples pour la liberté, la justice et la dignité, l'exaltation de l'amour, de la tolérance et de la solidarité entre les peuples.

Dan Mbo Kuba est né et grandi à Kinshasa en République Démocratique du Congo. Il est diplômé en Administration et Commerce, mais aussi d'un degré en Finance et Développement. Ses histoires traitent de l'humanisme et sont divertissantes, vivantes et intéressantes. Son tout dernier ouvrage est un Roman qui s'intitule << THE MISSING PIECE>>, lequel a été publié aux Éditions Jambo depuis septembre 2024. Il a été lauréat du tout dernier concours poétique sur la Passion - Liberté -Renaissance aux éditions la voix du livre / Yaoundé (Cameroun) suite à son texte au-delà des défis.

Artiste écrivain, poète et slameur ; **Fraubi Amel** est l'un de ces auteurs africains qui se bat pour une véritable paix au périple de sa vie. Auteur de trois recueils, il aborde aisément les thèmes liés à la vie et à la mort, à la politique et à tous ces maux qui minent le monde en général, et l'Afrique en particulier ; selon lui : l'Afrique est UNE et INDIVISIBLE. Très présent sur la scène continentale, il est pour le combat de la femme et promeut l'amour d'où son slogan : « Que Vive l'Amour... »

Athanase N.KANE est né le 20 décembre 1985 à Sittigo (commune de Séguénéga) au Nord du Burkina Faso, il enseigne le français au Lycée Yamwaya de Ouahigouya. Passionné de littérature depuis le Petit Séminaire de Koudougou, il est auteur d'un recueil de poèmes intitulé Les Morsures de l'existence, Editions Plum'Afrik, 2025. Outre l'écriture et l'enseignement, il s'intéresse aux métiers du cinéma et de l'audiovisuel. Dans une Afrique en plein chantier, ce poème qu'il soumet fait un constat : celui d'une jeunesse plutôt léthargique qui rêve d'aventure au-delà de la Méditerranée, d'où ce « Son de sirène ».

Mondo Kobi Arnold est un poète, écrivain et scientifique congolais, né à Kinshasa, capitale de la République Démocratique du Congo. Il est diplômé en Latin et Philosophie, aussi Licencié en Relations internationales à l'Université de Kinshasa. Amoureux de la science et de la littérature et auteur de plusieurs poèmes et œuvres scientifiques. Sa passion dans la poésie date depuis son enfance. Sa poésie est marquée par une emphase sur l'humanisme, le vouloir vivre ensemble avec un accent particulier sur l'amour, la justice et la solidarité.

Wankpo Franck, né le 30 juin 1998 à Zogbodomey, titulaire d'un baccalauréat série A1, a fait des études de Lettres à l'Université d'Abomey-Calavi.

Maria Manuel Godinho Azancot de Menezes filha de Manuel Pedro Azancot de Menezes e Maria de Lourdes Pires Godinho, nasceu em Portugal, vive em Angola, é médica. Tem editados em Portugal 101 poemas no livro "Lua Mágica", 102 poemas no livro "Voo Colorido"; Participou em Antologias Portuguesas, no Libero America- Africa Journal, no Best New Africain Poets (de 2017 a 2024) e em 2025 no African Poetry Anthology Chapbook,Vol 1.Usa uma linha de escrita livre e considera não ter influências literárias. Transparente e versátil, os poemas recheiam-se também de simbolismos e filosofia, numa escrita de sensibilidade, inconformismo, denúncia, esperança, amor- explosões de sensações como uma onda que alicia o Mundo.

Orlando Mussaengana: REY MATAKA VII é Orlando Jorge Mussaengana, Advogado, Escritor, Gestor Cultural e Curador literário (Chimoio/Moçambique, 1978). Foi Assistente jurídico no Gabinete do Conselho de Administração da Rádio Moçambique (2011/2018), Delegado da RM-Gaza (2018/2024), Locutor-Jornalista, Sonoplasta e Maquetizador na Rádio Encontro, Jornal Lúrio, MONASO, Direcção dos Antigos Combatentes e RM-Nampula (1998/2010). Publicou: ENCONTROS NEGROS - *Antologia Intrínseca* (2023); *MUTHEPO no poço das almas* (2023); *52 SUSSURROS D'AVÔ - Contos e Fábulas* (2024). Antologias: *Pontos e Versos - Uma antologia Multiverso*, Brasil/2024; *Meu Sonho de Amor*, São Paulo/2025; *Querida Mamã*, Mapeta Editora, Beira/2025, PONTES DE CIDADANIA – *Antologia de Contos e Crónicas da CPLP pro-Ambiente*, ETAH Editora/2025.

Jéssica Samara: Jéssica Samara é escritora e poetisa moçambicana. Atualmente reside em Maputo e escreve histórias e obras em português abordando temas como romance, esperança e sentimento genuíno, com uma escrita leve e cativante. Acredita que o que transforma um amador em artista é a sua mente idealista.

Gerson Leonardo Matusse: Nasceu em 2005, na Matola, Moçambique. Escreve poesia e contos. É estudante de Filosofia na Universidade Pedagógica de Maputo. Tem poemas publicados na "I Antologia Poética" (2024) da Nuvem de Letras e na antologia "Palavras sem Fronteiras" (2024), Organizado pelo brasileiro Renato Chagas.

Lorna Zita: É escritora, roteirista é autora de obra raízes e gritos que exploram temas como identidade, memória e resistência, É membro da Mwasa (National Writer Association of South Africa) e membro fundador do Círculo Académico de Letras e Artes de Moçambique. Representou Moçambique no festival BBC Contains Strong Language realizado no Reino.

Jaime Fernando Sigaúque: Nasceu aos 12 de Fevereiro de 2000, em Manjacaze, província de Gaza. Começou o seu trajecto artístico em 2016, na 11ª classe impulsionado pelo programa Batalha dos Nigas, da TV Sucesso. Em 2022 começou a escrever cânticos, na igreja e surgiu a ideia de declamar as letras e alguns cânticos, e desde lá vem apresentando poesias em alguns eventos na igreja, e só em 2023 com a problemática da tensão pós-eleitoral teve o impulso de começar a fazer poesia de cunho social.

Introduction by Tendai Rinos Mwanaka

In our 11th year we continue with the Best New African Poets anthology series which we begun in 2015. Last year we took a breather and did anniversary issues. But this year we return back with *Best New African Poets 2025 Anthology*.

This anthology has 75 poets from Africa and her disporas, over 185 poems dealing with a gamut of issues; governance, politics, love, relationships, spirituality, death, community, individuality. Each poet mirrored what his or her society is going through. We see poets in Nigeria dealing with strife and corruption, strife to do with Boko horam and the terrorits to the north, the Fulani cattle herders, the arguments which we see in the medias on the North versus South fractitous relationship, and the general agnst against the politicians. We have poets writing from Botswana, Tanzania, Malawi, Zimbabwe, Ghana, Nigeria, South Africa, Kenya, Uganda, Mozambique, Angola, Sao Tome, DRC, Niger, Burkina Feso etc in this anthology. With Malawi based poets very visible in this anthology as we don;t usually publish a lot of poems from Malawi.

We also have more new poets that previous contributors, meaning our project is still very much relavant and doing its job, giving new poets a platform to publish and grow. We still believe that adage, it takes 10 years to build a poet, so in the next ten years we will strive by all means to keep this platform open so that we raise another group of young poets like we did for the previous 10 years in the previous anthologies in which we gave space to over 1000 African poets.

We welcome you to *Best New African Poets 2025 Anthology*, and hope you will enjoy and get challenged by poetry in this offering.

Introdução por Lorna Zita

A Antologia BNAP 2025 pertencente aos escritores da lusofonia é o reflexo da força criativa de poetas que ousam transcrever no papel as suas dores e resistências. Este encontro literário reúne vozes de diferentes geografias que, com autenticidade, exploram temas universais e particulares, criando um mosaico poético que ultrapassa fronteiras.

Os poemas aqui reunidos abordam questões diversas: desde a luta pela liberdade, identidade e justiça social até às reflexões íntimas sobre amor, solidão, memória, natureza e espiritualidade. Cada texto revela um olhar singular sobre o mundo, mas também partilha uma vontade comum de transformar experiências individuais em matéria poética que ecoa no colectivo.

A temática da resistência surge em múltiplas camadas seja na evocação da força interior, no questionamento das tradições ou na denúncia de injustiças sociais. Da mesma forma, o amor e a perda aparecem como fios condutores que ligam sensibilidades humanas distintas, oferecendo tanto consolo quanto reflexão.

Em muitos dos poemas, nota-se ainda uma profunda ligação à herança africana, resgatando símbolos, fábulas e memórias históricas, que dialogam com os desafios do presente. A poesia surge, assim, como espaço de reconstrução e como ponte entre passado, presente e futuro.

Mais do que uma coletânea, esta Antologia 2025 afirma-se como um espaço de partilha, resistência e celebração da palavra, reunindo diferentes vozes numa mesma esfera literária, unidas pelo poder transformador da poesia.

untitled dub poem I
Aryan Kaganof

> *"The gods die differently in different societies."*
> *Lewis Nkosi*

Because you too will die, eventually,
be grateful for every breath.
Because you too will fail, eventually,
be grateful for every success.
Because you too will despair, eventually,
be grateful for every minor victory.
Because you too will hate and be hated, eventually,
be grateful for any signs of love, given or received.
Because you too are me, eventually,
be grateful for me, as I
am grateful for you.

untitled dub poem II
Aryan Kaganof

They urged the people to stay in their homes
But the people had no homes
They urged the people
to wear gloves and masks
But the people had no hands
Had no mouths
They urged the people
to keep their distance
But there was no space
Between the people
They urged the dying to breathe in and out
But the dying people had no air
And even those with air
Had no lungs
They urged the markets
To self-regulate
They urged the airlines
To levitate
They urged the virus
To go back where it came from
Finally they urged their mirrors
to stop reflecting
They were tired of seeing
How empty they were

untitled dub poem III
Aryan Kaganof

While we stayed home
doing the right thing
Watching Netflix and not boozing
They rounded up the homeless
Street people they called them
Cleaned up the streets they called it
For their own good they said
They put them in a camp
For their own good
without matresses
For their own good
Without masks or social distancing
For their own good
Without blankets or soap
For their own good
While we stayed home
doing the right thing
Watching Netflix

Who will they round up next?
For their own good
Will it be the dissenters?
Will it be the conspiracy theorists?
Will it be those who could not afford to pay their rent?
Will it be you?

Because of something you can't imagine yet
that you're not allowed to do?
Will it?
Think about that
While you stay at home
Doing the right thing
Watching Netflx and not boozing

Grief Residues
Victor Unachukwu

At 10:45 pm, the day after Democracy Day,
while rain isolated
the Benue state residents to their homes,
the Fulani Herdsmen sneezed through
a nearby police station, found their way
into the marrow of Yelwata town.
You think they would be in a hurry.
They dawdled into all the rooms, making sure
 to leave something: but first, a coppery metallic
 from blood & iron-rich organs, a remnant of ashes
 that raises your eyebrows, a way of saying,
"You are welcome to my world,"
103 bone fragments fire couldn't decay.
For some of the rooms, wrappers formed a brick,
a foundation for each body, which pulsates
 a chiming dial to heaven in the body of smoke.
In some stores, smoked bodies were lost
 in rice mounds, with charred flesh and boiled fat.
At the front steps, lay maggots perched
on clotted blood, which turned
to loamy soil &15 skulls of children
left with black holes.

How Do You Spell Home
Victor Unachukwu

when you pray to God
for what other countries give to their citizens?
Your country fights insecurity with prayer
 to God of Israel while Israel is fighting theirs
with weapons and technology.
now shift your eyes to your right:
You will see a leaking basket
dripping with blood.
You are clapping while standing in a
cemetery built on white blood.
 The only reason is you haven't
seen what you really are inside
your lover's armor, I swear.

Across a tard road, a woman riding
on a bike past a cemetery, her fingers
pointing at the graves of her husband
and brother, whose skins have peeled
away into chunks. The rider, in a biting
remark, suggests the cemetery is already
looking abandoned and should be renovated
 and "named after The Farnese Bull."
Or better still, "the president."

On grammar of Survival
Victor Unachukwu

How do I convince you that the Aba Women Riot of 1929
was Ogu Umunwaanyi, a fight to stay alive among
Bengal tigers and Hyenas?
That a hand of fellowship sneaked into our homes
to overwrite our grammar, religion, & dress
 at the time only to dig so many oilwells with
 the body dust & the trader's elbow heat.
My naked grandmother struts
on the streets of Umuahia, Bende District, Oloko,
 with pond fonds with which she ducked her ears
 against any halt or pause. She told us that after the
baby-protest which eventually matured into
a riot, many Warrant Chiefs resigned, the
first time women passed from
the kitchen to feminine enlightenment,
a time when a lot of men had lost faith in their wives.
What is jail like? an alleged father would ask.
"A jail is like a summer camp," a uniformed man would answer.

An Awakening of Souls
Okolo Chinua

From the turnaround of seas seen I found an envelope halfspread.
It read 'what comes in remains, trapped.'
I took it for a mouth with enclosed speech that came too far...
In the fire of its belly a root cultivates,
Not all give life when shook so I rise, an emblem for mirrored transects.
In the evening I am a buffalo in flight, existential on weighted transits with beliefs higher than the sky...
In my dreams I am a falcon carrying truth and gospel...
That what stays high need not come down....

From scarves beneath eyes flames find life.
A traveller finds a spot hunched, his breath an encapsulation of belief.
You find him with worry, your mind a ruminant starving.
What prowls in the dark seeks...
And why does the bird scream if not to be seen...
These tires spin into smiles, toothpasting matched memories...
In the liver of being is a cross, a ladder and smoke...
Nothing stays longer than sadness...
A memory of tears fickle and your mind lights, a fed damsel in deep water...

From the dead I awaken, full of life...

As a Comma Gliding through torn Edifices
Okolo Chinua

At the cliffs of madness sense sits.
My mind crawls through edifices memorising faces and beings.
The drums from the sky awaken and the clouds lose the weight they've carried.
The zincs on my forehead mirror the sadness within and every breath is a chore executed.
The windows in my palm fill the spaces left by dreams.
This testament, a billboard for proclamation.
With open eyes are tires running out of frustration,
Like a shepherd devouring a flock....

Everyday I awaken with doubts and doubts..
There's a trickle for every time these thoughts prowl.
In the process I become a moving comma, a circumcision of mistakes..
Half the time I rise like an umbrella, shield to all with beatings for praise...
And everyday I wear this smile still, an echo from a perforated door.
There are gaps in these sockets, like hollows in rooms building cobwebs.
Sometimes I'm a line drawn across the field, a mat for steps.
What becomes of a ball kicked... a lullaby for seven calling themselves kings.
When I pray it's not in expectation, it's to remind myself that words too can be said.

This weight in silence fans around crafting ripples of phlegm...
There's nothing here but dreams, hopes and glasses slipping from shaky hands.
On my lips are whispers, that the day I breathe my last I do so a god with wings for brackets.

A Declaration of Intention
Okolo Chinua

There are days I find myself submerged in memories I'd rather forget.
Like that goodbye made soon, the smile rather held, the hug rather kept.
Being human is a cycle of never growing, of making wrong choices and rationalizing them...
When I close my eyes it's all the love I've lost flooding, a whirlpool of storms.
I've never known how to hold so every evening I burn and arise at mornings cold all over.
This sun doesn't bring warmth so with duty I force myself to run my own mind.
I see terror, like a three year old in an elevator for the first time.
And "All I have loved I have alone" ...
It's morning and this cycle returns...

How do you define desire..
A turnaround, or a memory sucked in?
A whisper or a goodbye rushed?
Mine is a flower sprinting, a rotation of roses in storms and thorns for embrace.
These hands are weary, I've carried too much to hold still...
I tear every part from me to clothe yet with my pieces you stab me.
I show you this world and you give another.

On days I keep you warm you reward me with frost.
The day I wash you off it won't be with water, it would be with skin peeled off to bleed away all I've attached thanks to you.
The day I let go of you it won't be with sweet wine, charm and milk, it'll be with vitriol, spiel and bursts...
And with a full heart, I'll wish you the worst...

Always this internal struggle with loneliness
Abigail George
(for my brother)

I can see his pain. I want to tell him it is like Joseph's
coat, that it's a gift, but I don't feel brave enough.
I'm devoid of courage. He is a broken man struggling
with being kind and good and strong for his partner
and children. He is living on the edge of the world. Aren't
all men broken, and some women, the lonely kind?
Oh, I can see his pain. I can hear the struggle and
the honesty in his voice as his tears fall down his cheeks.
But I do not know how to acknowledge it. How to
give it shape and form in my hands. There is always
my internal struggle with loneliness, and about how
I am at a loss and cannot give this too shape and
form in my hands. I think I can only betray the people
that I love. I used to think that darkness was a gift like
a rain cloud or bloodless grass on a hot summer day
because it too came with light, but then the depression
scared it away and all I could do was stare at my face
in the mirror as the sun hovered and tried to placate
me. Now I listen to the pianist Olga Scheps, the composer
Maurice Ravel, and I study books, people and the
words of Joseph Brodsky. In other words, I am supposed
to know better, I am supposed to do better and write
love poems to myself. I am supposed to be a Judson
Jerome or a Yehuda Amichai but now that the man is gone I am
finally equipped to love him, and the only men left

in my life is my father and brother so now I love and
forgive them instead. Isn't that what lonely women
do when the wave threatens to engulf them? I too have
pain but of this I say nothing to the men in my life
because they won't understand how to deal with it, how to handle
it. If I write about the war in my head and that I carry in
every cell in my body since the man left I will be alright, I tell
myself. This is my story. My origin story. I am not a storyteller
for nothing. I can see my pain. It has turned me into a disciple.
I can see pain. The man is no longer in my life for a
reason, I tell myself and I will myself to believe this. I can
still remember when the man traced my ribs with his fingers.

When you came into my life
Abigail George

What is a river?
Is it made up of fish spit?
Something to hold a body?
Something to hold a thing?

I fold joy
a blanket of sea
into the wildflowers
of my heart

I know what hurts my spirit
You don't
I fill a vase with raw crests,
the metaphysical,
a lake
drained of bronze,
tinder

You wave me away
Only want your father
I am blood
I am ancient
I am wave

Sleeper, you're like a magnet

Your Blippy
Your Elmo
Your Teacher Rachel
They're all wise
too wise for me
You are my Woolf
You are my wolf
Your skin as pale
as pale as the wind
My father tells me
to keep writing

He is beginning to disappear
So am I
So am I

Can you feel my loneliness?
Can you see it?

To two female poets, one Israeli and another Palestinian, from a South African poetess
Abigail George

I sip hot chai tea
while my mother
buys lettuce and tomatoes
for our lunch
I arrange
the frangipani
on my desk
with the aorta
in the middle
I sit at my desk, writing
"I see you",
"I want to remember you,
your hands,
your wrists,
your fingers,"
"It's important
that I remember
all of you"
There's a war outside my window
an ocean away
I need evidence
access to a language
that I can speak fluently
Evidence of the milky way,
constellations and young galaxies,

humanity and the universe
I need trust, I ache for solutions
that I find in holy books
sacred texts, knowledge from wise men
And then I think
of all the mornings
The morning coffees
I never had
with you, mother,
and my sister
I think to myself
will a ceasefire ever be realised
The day my brother hit me
I wrote a poem for Palestine
I carried it in my heart
In bone
In smoke
In flesh
In my pocket, under my sleeve
I carried it like the air
in a prison
carries noise pollution
I was still of the belief
that men could change
I was a monster
He was a monster
We had turned
into a family of monsters overnight
Stillness and energies of noble origins

trial that does not burn,
tribulation made of dust
but that tastes of gold
Palestine
you're a diamond-jewel that shines bright
in the night sky
that rises up
to meet the moonlight,
the inner man, the spirit man,
the guide, the shaman
the multitude of stars
and milky way your companion
veins and blood
in the grave
restored in
sunrise and sunset
the coffin carries a wildflower
not a lamentation
no abyss in the eyes
it's a new arrival in eternity
new love
new seed
a snail's novel earth
When my brother hit me
at that exact moment
the ancestors spoke to me
of violence, extreme anguish,
bitter medicine, the pills I am ashamed to take
and sadness, the futility that comes

with the label of outsider
His anguish, his label
Whatever is planted in earth
satisfied
sad with stories
myth that we were led astray by once
Whatever is planted near rain
even this is God's doing
God's choice
grief is just a new beginning
Whatever grows in seawater
even the trees
even reefs and bridges
plateaus and landscapes
the genius of mammals
understand you too have wings
understand this barrier to the soul
the wolf knows chronic stress
the bird knows invincible birdseed
they understand this kind
of knowledge
of gratitude
that comes from Spartacus
other revolutionary fighters
Maybe I was planted
in the wrong place
wrong home
wrong career
wrong illness

Maybe I was planted
with the wrong mother
with the wrong father
with the wrong sister
wrong brother
for I did not find
ochre and rust
moving pictures of happiness
or lilies of beauty there
only longing
and regret
longing for things
that never seemed
to find me
Maybe I grew
like a tree
too sturdy
not sturdy enough
Perhaps I will grow
into a prosperous silhouette
Perhaps I will know
prestige, orient myself in the home
in my bones
I will discover Atlantis and doppelganger,
the witness that is also the fugitive
Maybe I asked
too many questions
of God
of a mother

who never
made the time
to listen to me
Maybe I didn't
wear makeup
enough
loved myself
too little
not enough
the wolf knows
the bird knows
they understand this kind
of ingratitude
I think of this clove
that soothes my toothache
I need to stop thinking
of the pain I'm in
garum masala in the pot of curry
cardamon
this tea I am drinking
how it improves
my consciousness
lightens my being
I remember war
It's as if it's inhabiting another realm
another planet
It's as if a spiritual
conquest has to take place
as well as forced removals

Why, God?
Why?
I turn to poetry.

AFRICAN WOMAN
Vihje ben Nkhunga

Until you perceive
the aroma
of her delicacies
in the kitchen
You will have
no reservations

Until you caress
Her waist beads
Under the light of the crescent
moon
You will have
no reservations

Until the tip
of her pointed breast tits
prick your bare chest
And send your brains
to mount kilimanjaro
You will have
no reservation

Until you test
the horny
that drips

from her succulent lips,
Sweet horny
like Shire valley horny combs,
You will have
no reservation

Until she wriggles
her waist for you
to the sound of Chisamba drums
At the market square
On the rite of passage day
You will have
no reservation

Until you escort
her from the well
with her clay pot
balanced on her head,
Her broad dark bare shoulders
challenging the October sun
You will have
no reservation

Until she kneels
before your uncles
with her face down,
Dimples shining on her cheeks
A smile through her diastema
An animal print wrappers

swallowing her curvy feet.
You will have
no reservation.

When God Sat Beside Me It was a quiet revelation in the hush of dawn
Athalia Pule

I thought You left
Truly, I did
In the thick of my sorrow
when the nights stretched
like unanswered prayers
and my mind knelt
under weight I couldn't name
But You were there
not in thunder
nor in scripture shouted
from pulpits I couldn't enter
but in breath
In the steady rhythm
of being held
by something unseen
I did not see the burning bush
but I saw the flame
flicker in my chest
when I almost gave up
and didn't
You were there
when I walked through Psalms again,
this time not bleeding
When I read Isaiah
and finally believed

You make beauty from ashes
and not the other way around
There were no miracles
no sea parted
no stone rolled away
but the chains rusted
and my hands began to open.
Grief became a garden,
and doubt a path
that still led home
I see now
that healing did not come
all at once
it was Ruth in the fields
gleaning hope
grain by grain
It was Elijah fed by ravens
sustained in unexpected ways.
It was You
in every breath
I thought I took alone
So now
I light my candle
not to keep the dark away
but to remember
You were there
when I could not see.
And maybe
this is faith

not the absence of ache,
but the presence
of You
in the ache
The knowing that
even in silence,
even in the stillness
of no answers,
You sat beside me
And You never left.
Butterfly Whispers.

Rock bottom
Athalia Pule

Rock bottom is not a fall
it is a landing
A sudden silence after too many screams
echoing through the chambers of the self
It is a room with no doors
just mirrors that never reflect the same face twice.
I have arrived
Not as a visitor
but as a resident of my own ruin
There is no applause here
only the quiet ticking
of a clock that mocks me with its patience
Hope is a language I no longer speak.
It died somewhere between
"maybe tomorrow" and "what's the point?"
Now I speak only in sighs and half-finished prayers
They said the bottom would teach me
But all I've learned
is how to sit with emptiness
until it stops feeling like a stranger
Some nights, I speak to God
as if He still lives here
but the ceiling does not answer
and the silence is so loud
I begin to mistake it for truth
I miss myself

but I don't remember who that was
Only fragments
a laugh that once belonged to me
a dream I used to water
before the drought came
If I am still alive
it is out of habit
not desire
I breathe
because my body has not yet learned how to stop.
Rock bottom is a room.
And I—I have folded myself into the floorboards,
waiting for either resurrection
or rest

The heart pines
Athalia Pule

Is it a heart if it doesn't pine for you,
A hollow chamber echoing with the ghosts of what could be?
A mere organ, pumping blood through veins
Yet devoid of the ache that makes it whole
The sweet torment of longing and the exquisite pain of desire
What is a heart, if not a vessel for dreams unfulfilled
A fragile thing, teetering on the edge of madness
A metronome of solitude marking time in silence
And I wonder in this aching void
Is it still a heart, or merely a shadow of what love could be
So tell me, love, if absence be the test
Is it a heart or merely a jest
Reminding me that to love is to suffer
To yearn is to be alive, yet to be alive is to ache
What cruel jest is this that the heart should crave
What it cannot possess, a fruit forever out of reach
I am but a marionette strings pulled by the whims of fate
So I ask again is it still a heart if it doesn't pine for you?
A question that gnaws at the very marro
w of my existence...

Shore of Eternity
Muhammad Ghazali

If I look at the crystal moon
All stars that twinkle in Milky Way
The gaiety eloquence of cock at dawn
The bright rise and golden sunset
Or the pregnant sun at its zenith
It deems and blinks my soul sight

If I dream of heaven, its rosy bay
The innocence in infant faces asleep
The tenderness in lovers fancy faces
The bless solitude of bridal night
The rainy conducive lightening May
It shatter the trouble deep within

You're the sweet heaven in me
The sound earth I live within
The oxygenated particle I do breathe
There, they seem to tell all our sorrow
In few wild words they tend to borrow
Here we meet at the shore of eternity

Where My Heart Is?
Muhammad Ghazali

Where my heart is?
In a deep Blue vale sea
Pretence eyes in heaven
Dark August clouded sky
A hot starry summer night

Where my heart is?
Rattles at tattered dirty space
Tangles a frozen winter haze
Mantles a melting amber snow
Dangles in lips marry and gay

Where my heart is?
In dessert Caravans thirst
Anarchy of starved aged lion
Sharp lens of an Arabian eagle
Or brotherhood of mankind

Where my heart is?
Here either, nor there
Though it lost no sanity
It strides somewhere
This heart everywhere

Nightmare
Muhammad Ghazali

Hark! Ghoul emerges in dark
Hungry of flesh, thirsty of blood
Bold and moves in cyclone
Like mad man chasing nothing
Come close, retreat, retrieve
Safe wall does crack, door ajar
Esoteric voice calling in new names
Hark! It echoes in a strange tongue
Distant, distinct, complex, complete

The angry ghoul in my view
Betrayed, heavy heart pounds
Stomach heavenly groans
Tick, tick, tick wall whispers
Wish I'm dead not only bed
It seems to lose common sense
Towards me it rushes. Whop!

A kitten in a corner meow
Dearest Kitty eaten, dead and gone
Nightmare, horror, terror in a mirror
Timing skips, Tonight at Night
Voices, silence but pulse beat
Reveals dead, I in the dark
Groans, ghoul dragging edible me
Smears in blood as I scream

Terrible, night dashes through
A tap, on shoulder, "wake up" a voice
Heart still pounds, Heaven be thank
Happy this divine dawn, It's a nightmare!

Northern Africa Nations
Ivan Gaćina

There's no greater pain
than the one which a man inflicts on another
disrupting his generous hospitality
with "Trojan" in a hate cellophane.
A sword of fate destroys the tissue of life
with hellish forces fanning the destructive flames
while the forests swallow millions of heroes,
and colonizers dishonor our women
and enslave our children.
Why are you digging graves for us, our British brother,
while shedding rivers of blood in Africa?
Black days have wrapped our homes with a veil of sadness
while the desolate land is visited by temptation.
While we feed the pain with peace,
hunger with love, thirst with patience
the Shakespearean question "To be or not to be"
shelters the African continent.
We clear new roads alongside our ancestors' graves
hoping the rain will wash away the injustice
and a new day will bring freedom.
At least that is what our dreams allow us to do
and we owe so much to the future generations,
since no matter how hard we are oppressed,
we believe it's our duty to be better and more humane beings.

Whispers In The Night
Abigail Vanessa Bwakila

You found me in the dark forest
Entangled in thorns of confusion
I'll admit, I was not at my best
You threw me a lifeline
You listened, understood, you knew exactly what I felt
How could I not be mesmerised by you

You opened up a world of doom
A world of sadness
All the while drawing me in
I fell in love with it
A welcomed destruction

We were never meant to last
We bent and then we broke
The darkness that consumed you, a comfortable cloak
My shiny impediment
All my patience, you spent
And yet this lost soul engulfed deeper into the vast

A garden watered in salty tears
Can only birth malignance
Did I know I would pay the price in advance?
A self-inflicted wound
The self I envisioned already doomed
So to the garden I took some shears

Perhaps I revelled in such gloom
Perhaps you were my dark companion
Two dark spirits dancing in the night- a joyous reunion
But your despair outweighed mine
Yours simmered throughout the years- a most intoxicating wine
I leaned too much towards the light, I assume

I left the forest scratched and scathed
But you remain
I could not fathom this choice insane
The light burned you upon contact
You did not want to be saved, so finally I cracked
I saved myself. Shed my scarred carcass. You were not fazed

I walked toward the blinding light
Hacked away the whispering thorns
Decided to walk in darkness no more
And still you stay. But whatever for
You bear the curse, the burden of sight

Labyrinth
Abigail Vanessa Bwakila

I am in a labyrinth constantly chased by a minotaur
The ground beneath quivers with its horrendous snore
It plagues me all day yet strangely allows me reprieve under the blanket of the stars
At the greeting of first light it is on my heels
It thumps its chest and roars and the earth quakes
The rain comes and then the blistering sun
And all the while I tremble and I break and I run
The noise is deafening. It penetrates my every pore
The silence is even worse. For it brings the promise of its existence but not the knowledge of its location
My one companion- my soul I released from its mortal chains
No such thing could survive in a frame with desolation beating through its veins
The sound of my recoiling became an all too familiar song
The tapping of my bare feet an all too welcome destruction
It demands a purging. A surrender. A sacrificial purification
Before my acute and utter annihilation
I feel it's breathe hot behind my neck
The stench of death itself. My passage into oblivion
I turn to face my fate. The minotaur is me

Mirror This, Mirror That
Abigail Vanessa Bwakila

If I were to hold up a mirror
With legs and a mouth and hands to boot
Would you gaze lovingly at he/she or at your jerkish feet?
Mirror this, mirror that, mirror this and that

The social battery
The number one killer of men
The number one confidence robber
Pssh, stop the flattery
The social battery
The number one shame monger of women

In the morning bright and early
Affirmation in mind, I dance
I dance with myself before I ever ask for accompanying hand

If I told you what I see
Would you then find in me a true friend as well?
If I solemnly swore to see you, would you in turn see me?
The clock strikes 25:00
My shift's began, your potent self-reflection I was to guard and boastfully defend

Years swept by now on the back of Iris's stork
In your hands I place a fiery peacock
The bells ring- the clock strikes none

If I were to hold up a mirror now
Would you converse with him or her?

Would you reward his/her patience?
Her growth, his journey to discover his voice?
Would you applaud her choice?
The social battery
Bad business for you if you let the world tell you who you are
Little girl, little boy, grown woman and man
Oh precious you are a burning hot, bright light imbued star
Storks came from near and far
Peacocks, Iris, Thot and a fleet, convoy and a battalion

And if I told you what I see
Would you smile?
Would you frown?
Would you hear me?
A beacon in dreary times, I see you from but a mile
Enough of that- Now, chest out Fix your crown

On Words Refusing to Die
William Khalipwina Mpina

I sat, surrounded by vigilant pairs of eyes,
And I wrote something on the ground.
The words were hidden and unexplained,
A mystery to those around.

Words are what they are,
Unchanging and unwavering.
People wear their masks,
Concealing their true selves.

But life is fragile and fleeting,
And cannot be easily defined.
I thought I had written these words,
Yes, of course!

Even After We're Gone
William Khalipwina Mpina

Even after we're gone,
The world will breathe again
Horizons kissed by dawn,
Skies painted in colours unseen.

There will be others,
footprints on paths we've walked,
voices weaving prayers
to God.
There will be love,
gentle as rain-soaked petals,
and hope, a flame that never fades,
lighting the way through dark nights.

Yes, there will be poverty,
but hands will outstretch
to lift and heal.

For even after we're gone,
The world will carry on
a drum of dreams,
where hope endures.

This Graveyard Called My Country
William Khalipwina Mpina

Like a parliament of silence,
This graveyard called my country
Is where my bones shall lay.

My bones are fallen flags of a forgotten revolution,
After a fierce battle with disease.
My bones are a bureaucracy of decay,
Aching with the weight of promises,
Stinking of treaties signed in blood and broken by time.

My bones are a cage for the echoes of speeches,
Like a nation of shadows.
In this graveyard,
My bones will lie beneath the soil of a system
That fed on my marrow, carved its laws into my skeleton,
And left me to fight alone.

On a clear Day ….
Lucas Zulu

    You can eye a lizard content
just to lie on the rocks of the veld
    here every minute so, you can hear a voice
             of Limpopo River, burbles over
                  the rocks, a song
                      that soften
                        a heart
                        of marble,
                    a
                    serpentine
                river
                  winds
                      through
                  the village,
                  like
                a languid
                    python,
              its
            tranquil
            surface
            mirroring
            the blue,
                as it slithers
                    and crawls
                        as if its going
                            nowhere,

silently.

Bellum
Lucas Zulu

I guess you once live in the laisse faire society
  that was stunned by the violent scene
you had ne'er seen. As the plot thickens the press,
  the poets, the pacifist wont sensationalized
this bloody bellum and its impact. Its aftermath
  will bring every clam to its knees and this
would've effect on ordinary folks like us
  and the land where they keep on playing with fire
everything will turn into ash. I presume
  you'll seek to seize the cheek of surviving
the explosive devises, as a boy-child
  you'll be penned for a century for hurling
pig wheels armed to teeth with Molotov cocktails
  as a girl-child beads of sweat will breakout
on her weary brow, mortally petrified to pen
  an anti-war poem that won't see the light
you'll be expatriated in; you'll be allergic to strife
  I figured out the wee woo! wee woo! Ne'er stops,
the sobbing of fledglings ne'er stops, the wailing
  of skirts ne'er stops. And no drops of waterworks
will ever stop, this ocean of life fluid
  I haven't seen in days. It feels like the deep rift

will take ages to heal. The knotted artilleries exist
  just on paper like a strange vowel between
the alphabets that squeal and squeal for attention.
  I postulate you are eying this live on Facebook.
There's always Goliath who ride roughshod over
  the common herd and he shouldn't. Who finds comfort
and revenue, while the embittered folks tussle.
  The humiliated folks flee the burnt ground like ants.
The video doesn't blow up the story, everything
  that is ruined comes as a blow to citizens
the silent majority is on the margin of poverty line.

Sanctuary
Lucas Zulu

Sometimes, I walk out to the nearby veld,
where natures serenity recharges my soul.
The tranquility envelops me, calming my mind
and lifting the mental fog that swirled thickly
around my thoughts. Surrounded by the blue
and white squalls I breath in fresh air,
rich with floral scents,
with few heads around,
just the occasional herdsmen
and An alabaster flock of cattle egrets.
Its such a relief to hang out
in the peaceful atmosphere,
I feel a deep sense of relief wash over me,
as I sit amidst the grass lilies, the Highveld reeds
gentle choir fills the air, orchestrated by the breeze
subtle touch, its violins, violas and victors
sets the tambookie grass in motion,
its delicate blades swaying to the beat
soothing my thoughts.

Home
Bradley Nsukuzokuduma Moyo

Home is where the heart is,
Does that mean everytime
That I carry my feet I carry home?

Can I even escape
The weight of my father's dream,
My grandfather's legacy
And my mother's prayers?

Is it the same home that
I let in every Jil, Jane and Poe?

Home is a question of belonging
And I belong deeply to myself.

Home is the toothless smile of my grandmother,
Her wrinkled hand
pulling me close for a hug,
Saying welcome muzukuru*
Welcome home!

*mzukuru -Shona word for grandchild or nephew.

In Between
Bradley Nsukuzokuduma Moyo

In between her boobies
titties-tats
(You call them breasts)
Is a place of rest.

Her embrace is a smell of home
Saying;
" come,come
Return unto me."

Am I talking about your mother
 or your ex
That exiled you to places
of not coming back?

*Tichaona mangwana *
But here we are in these foreign embraces
Of a land refusing to take us as we are.

Tichaona mangwana * - we will see tomorrow.

the fisherman
Archie Swanson

this morning saturated flats were open to the sky
perforated here and there with mud prawn holes

but now… last rays on distant hills
he has returned with rod in hand to try his luck

lone hunter on a breathless edge
where mirror meets the matted sedge

along the line of surging tide he'll cast his bait into the wild
and hope that there's a bite before the fading of the light

the inky black
Archie Swanson

the sleepers and the steely track
the buffer stop
no junction here or signalman
no point to switch this train along or back

no stationmaster nor porter here
no first-class dining car
no bathroom door
just cattle trucks and fear

this is the final stop
the journey's end
a single fare
no option of return

a one-way ride
a terminating train
the end of line
the end of time

the shower room
the Zyklon B
the chimney stack
the inky black

punting the Cam
Archie Swanson

we pass beneath the Bridge of Sighs
breathing our hellos yet whispering goodbyes
a teenage punter has our ear as he lays his future bare
law at University College then on to private equity
not boxed in Canary glass but in Soho offices somewhere

both Bishops class of '73 – we imagine we'd have flourished here
Nicky with clever turn of phrase – first choice for every speech on special days
and me – fruit trader – surfer – poet I am told
at 69 we're getting just a little old
where once we moved with youthful pace we ambulate with stately gait

as proud parents punt past Trinity Hall on this graduation day
Nicky engages the Turkish student opposite
dark and willowy she takes to him immediately
he once chose Turkey as a subject for political affairs
and since seems drawn to all things Turkish unawares

earlier we visited Wren Library elevated to escape the floods of yesteryears
the book-lined hall recalls the academic prowess of this place
oracle to Newton's laws that launched us into space
beneath cabinet glass – carved walking stick with wizard head
and annotated Principia Mathematica once held in Newton's hand

the clanging pole returns me to the here and now
trimmed willow trees
the wizened bows
our furrowed brows
lined with libraries of thought and special emphases

no doubt this stream will call our callow punter back
when he as well has boring stories to be told
perhaps a captive lass subjected to his tale
of life that fell into his lap
or best-laid plans that failed

THE WIND KNOWS NOTHING
Emman Usman Shehu

If it has its way   the wind will
turn caution on its head   in a

display that easily spells
revelation   The wind knows

nothing about keeping secrets
under cover   as it blows

in any direction it chooses
like a free will

SHADOW'S PACE
Emman Usman Shehu

I am   the shadow's tread
soft   on dew-slick stone   long

before   the mark is seen
I trail   the warmth of steps

no haste   no falter
only   the weight of time

TALKING POINT
Emman Usman Shehu

The stalking   starts long before
the flourish of naming   long

before   the unhurried framing
long before   the nunc dimitis

that seals the rest in peace
a final   talking point.

Beauty on the road
Oscar Gwiriri

Driving along the Beitbridge highway,
I spotted a stranded beautiful woman
With a beautiful daughter almost twin.
Suddenly found my foot harsh on brakes,
Took an about turn for their rescue,
They had missed a bus to Polokwane,
Which had daughter's college luggage.

Suddenly I got them in my SUV car,
Suddenly I got grinding the wheel,
Hoping to catch the suddenly missed bus,
But the bus driver seemed to be giving
My truck a taste and my tank a waste.
It was rather a highway goose chase.

Just found myself at Beitbridge post,
Where the naughty driver parked to clear.
We embraced and bid farewell with a sigh,
Remembered I was supposed to be elsewhere.
But her beauty drove me insane to drive insanely.

The song
Oscar Gwiriri

I pity mother when she proudly sings
About Jerusalem being her heaven.
I must book her a tour to Jerusalem's
Hell Gate, Harod's Gate and Dung Gate.
Possibly she may demystify her vision
And the visionary milk and honey Canaan
Opiated in her mind by Colonial priests,
Who illusioned her to loathe our ancestors.
For surely, some day I will rescue mother
From the yoke of colonialism strategies,
Possibly she will sing a different song
Which she does not long to be at Zion Gate.

Love
Oscar Gwiriri

As he sighed with deep relief,
He pondered again and again,
On the opportunity cost
Of making love to her
Against his money she squeezes.

Zenzele Ndebele
Jabulani Mzinyathi

With the precision of a surgeon
A surgeon wielding a keen scalpel
You cut the gangrene of the lies
The lies peddled as our history
You deliver blows to the counterfeit story
Exposing that which was long hidden
They say that lies have very short legs
Zenzele Ndebele you deserve the accolades
The past , the present and the future indebted
A pat on the back for setting the record straight
Those propagandists fast put to shame
Those that claim to have liberated us by themselves
Those that now bask in the sunshine of self interest
The intensity of your gallantry plain to see

Desert
Jabulani Mzinyathi

We who have an extra abundance
An abundance of lustrous flora and fauna
We who boast of the mightily flowing Kasambabezi
And the stolen majestic Shungu na mutitima
And to the south the crocodile infested Vhembe
We who boast of those enigmatic mountains
There in the evergreen Eastern Highlands
We who boast of vaults brimming with gold
We who were blessed with alluvial diamonds
We who are blessed with birds of all plumage
Singing their alluring early morning songs
Now find immeasurable pleasure and succulence
Making some kind of pilgrimage to that desert
It is time to ask: Why are we stone blind?

Suits
Adiela Akoo

They lied! It's *not* the same!
You watch re-runs to reconcile
a semblance of reel and real life
To console and remind yourself
of the reason you started . . .

First to fade is the illusion of glamour:
you swop heels for flats
to parley with potholed pavements
and avoid flirty old men who've forgotten
their age . . . wisdom . . . and daughters

Sharks, sniffing fresh candidate meat
bet on how long it will take for you to break
The seasoned, lesser souled, sport perverse pleasure
in pushing you over the edge—
misery loves company!

But what *actually* breaks you is the two-year-old—
in court! And the others like her!
You no longer hold back tears as you tell me about it later

You should've seen her, you say
She's so cute. Innocent! *A baby!*
How could her father do that?

Within a space of two months, I helplessly watch you break
over and over and over again, surrounded by venomous vipers
in a hard, cruel, bitter, ruthless new world

I've raised you to be soft, kind, loving
I've raised you for a hopeful, better world
I've sheltered you. *Have I failed you?*

Nightly, I apply Arnica to ease back muscles pulled stiff under a
pile of files
saying silent, fervent, healing prayers over your heart chakra in the
process
and soothingly suggest soaking your sore feet in warm salt water

Your father urges you to leave this field saying it's quite okay to
quit!
He strengthens his case by mentioning all your classmates
who've already changed career course
But you've inherited your mother's stubborn resolve!
So I tell you about my aunts and *their* daughters who *also* cried
during articles when tender beauties had to face down hardened
criminals

'One is an ombudsman now
The second, a summa cum laude
opted to be part of a multinational
The third is an early-retired diplomat, once in charge
of the five islands, thereafter stationed in Paris. My point—

It *will* get better!

As for the sharks and vipers of the world, remember:
they're just people who've been hurt—and are still hurting
It becomes easier when you see them as that
But learn quickly how to avoid them bleeding on you!

I will teach you, if you pay close attention

Pain is a lesson—it hardens some and softens some
It takes a great deal of strength and wisdom
to choose softness after pain
Never mistake this softness for weakness. *It is powerful!'*

Until then, I say protective prayers handed down
to subdue ancient demons that stand alongside man
whispering hate and hostility into unsuspecting Hearts –
though some have hearts *already* diseased, or dead

As you walk through this perilous Valley of Death
I fervently pray that the Almighty walks with you
I fervently pray that you don't succumb
to the viperous venom…

THE WORLD OUTSIDE MY WINDOW
Adiela Akoo

Reclining on my sofa, gazing out my window, my thoughts are adrift on the breeze,
That gently sways through the nodding flowers and rustling leaves.
The greenery and lushness framed above and below by the azure of the pool and skies.
Oh Tranquility! What beauty to my eyes!

Some Hadedas arrive and begin meticulously prodding the earth,
Their greyness diminished by red and yellow robins splashing colour across this window's girth.
A giant tree along the fence forever reaching up, up, up to the Heavens,
Nature in all her splendour—a tribute to God!

Oh, to be but a leaf on that tree! With no cares in the world, no reckoning of good deeds nor bad,
No sense of loss, never ever being sad.
No bonds, no taxes, no worrying about crime,
No yesterdays, no tomorrows, in fact—no time!

If I could be but a leaf on that tree,
And of this encumbering world be free, be free!

I WILL KEEP YOU,BROTHER!
Ntensibe Joseph

When all is not sure of his destiny
When he moves in their crosshair
The dungeons are his home
And his mouth shut

Is it the *sun colours* he hugs
Or the stuffed wallet caked with dry plasma?

No, No
I will keep my brother.
I am my brother's keeper.
I will open my muzzle and bellow and remind my brother. Of the hurting
The aching, The bullying, The impunity, The pain
The pain:
The itching pain, The open wounds, The tears…

I will remind my brother
Of the emptiness , The Hopelessness, The murder
The killings,
The deaths…

Brother, wake up
Where is your heart

You have been skinned, you've lost your eyes Brother, *ephphatha*...
Our lands are no more
Our kins are dinning with the ancestors...

I am my brother's keeper I will tell him to wake up To keep hope
To rise up
To open your eyes
Get new flesh
Get your heart back

Come home brother...
See our open graves beckoning us,
Come see what we have become,
Come see the nothingness in the land, Come see the desert in the swamp,

Can't you see this could be my last you hear of me.... Brother, I want to keep you,
But can you?

ODE TO THE PILGRIM (*To the Pilgrim that never came back-* THE LITTLE DRUMMER BOY)
Ntensibe Joseph

Who is he that drums bow to?
Who is he that melodies worship?
Who are you that sounds adore?

You who massaged and caressed the drums.
You who the congregation stood still in 'uhs' and 'ahs'
You, through your drum smooches they worshipped their Creator

It was you that birds sung alongside,
The drums you stroked
It was you that the sun observed in silence and took a bow…

Wasn't it you that the old and young smiled?
Wasn't it you that survived
-almost
What we thought would take you?
Wasn't it you who had changed?
Wasn't it you??

And one Friday evening, Your creator
        Heard your drums…
He welcomed you to His choir
        I hope you play equally as good…

I WILL SUMMON MY GHOSTS
Ntensibe Joseph

I shall rouse my ghosts
and give them a tale:
First I'll feed them on the news of the land
They will then ask why trees stand no more
Why the wells are dry
Why grasses are burnt all the time
They will ask about their once fresh air!
And like an idiotic grandchild, I'll stare…
I know they will ask why
I fill their grounds with sewage
And why I cannot control my buttocks
And dump in one place.
They will ask why I trade my loins for loins.
Yes, they will ask about the loins market!
And my nuts they will grab and ask:
"Are these for trade?"
And I'll whimper in pain and anguish;
"Yeah! What we are left to do!"
Then my spirits shall rage
And facing my ghosts, I shall;
And quiz:
You, why be silent on us?
Yesterday and tomorrow!
Even now?

Why does father feed our neighbours
And starve us?
Why are we orphans with parents?
You have let these hyenas feed on us!
Do you drink the blood and devour the offals ?
Bajajja, who are we?
Did you take ourselves and left us with us?
Why are others not us?
Are we not of the same liquids and clay?
Are you listening?
Can you even hear me?
Answer me;
Can you hear me?

spirits/ghosts

I'LL FLY AWAY
Emmanuel Tumwesige

I came
I stayed,
I saw
And learned.
I did
Like you did
I laughed
You smiled
I thought
I was right
      Always.

                    Now you sit
                    While I do,
                    I smile
                    And cry
                    At once-
                    I'm muddled.
                    Where are you?

I dance
In mud
Your eyes
Are blind-
My eyes
Are wet

This world
Has changed
I'm crying
    All days.

        You're silent
        My icon,
        But know
        That my grave
        Awaits,
        I cannot stay
        And dance,
        The music
        Has changed
        They play
        Bull dyke.

WOLVES.
Abdullatif Khalid Eberhard

Peace of my mind stolen,
replaced by a piece of you,
not fitting my fledgling mind,
mounding me in two.

Masking my persona,
fear of being uncovered,
living with eyes averted,
scared you'll see right through.

Destruction became the option,
but hindsight cleared my view,
hurting myself never gave back,
peace of mind stolen by you.

So long I felt broken and lost,
healing didn't seem worth the cost,
having to deny the black wolf,
to feed the emaciated white.

Destruction became the option,
but hindsight cleared my view,
hurting myself never gave back,
peace of mind stolen by you.

Which.

Which one.
Which one survives?

The one you feed.

Which.
Which one.
Which one survives?

The one you feed.

Destruction no longer the option,
hindsight cleared my view,
loving myself gave back,
peace of mind I never knew.

Destruction no longer the option,
hindsight cleared my view,
loving myself gave back,
peace of mind I never knew.

Which one will you feed?

TO LILITH.
Abdullatif Khalid Eberhard

She wrote so dark her nose would bleed,
a crimson stain on her white, divine blouse.
She'd hum to the dark entities
flowing in and out of the house.

She barely ate, barely slept—
said the bed shook
when she dreamed of peace.
I nodded…
I understood—
but withheld belief.

She swore she was born
in the middle of life,
not young, not old—
just in time for it all to make sense…
and fall apart.

She owned my heart.

Never was pitch-blackness so perfectly poetic,
so uninterrupted—
I lived in her veins,
alongside the sunken ships
that rotted in her soul.

The life that scorched her
paid for it in full—
not in revenge,
but in its quiet regret
to make a person whole.

Even monsters
get to wash the blood away
in the water of God.
But she wore her blood like a dunce hat—
we all could see it,
honest as a treasure map.

She ended on unspoken words,
confused states of consciousness.
She'd have been better burned—
like the witches.

I'll miss her in Eden.
I won't tell Eve she was here.
As if she'd believe it.

I guess we're even.

LONDON BRIDGE IS FALLING
Orji Chidiebere

Great were their manipulations on us.
They held us down to our knees,
Blinking auras of false hopes and futurity
As they prey on our sensibilities

Africa, that ancestral warriors' land of greatness
Was conquered by the mediocrity in their words.
She was sold out by greed and our own vulnerabilities
They taught us to accept we were inferior

Those hydra-headed monsters of deceits
Came with their falsified holy books in one hand
And with the other hand, they stole our essences
Labelling us primitive in pretence and hypocrisy

Ask me of my traditions and cultural values.
We threw them away at their acculturation conference
Without proper syncretism, we fell to their traps
And became a testing ground for their dictatorial agendum.

Africa is a courageous lion, though wounded by their betrayals.
Her value cannot be tamed by their prejudices.
She emerges victorious as they still depend on her
To activate a world order of peace and continuity!

Today, we have our eyes glued to re-writing our history.
With these rising hopes, we've conquered their Euro-centricisms
And like Jericho, their walls are falling down
At the echo of Africa's rebirth!

Lazybones
Martin Chrispine Juwa

He lies on ribs
which clink like coins falling on rough floor.
The pain of hunger is piercing in his throat
and the rumbling voice of his stomach
seals the air around him.
The smell of tinned fish,
the aroma of cooking veggies,
and the grinding of dry cassava
nearly suffocates him.
He lies on his breaking ribs,
waiting to be fed, to be fed, by neighbours.
His eyes gaze at the empty Azure sky
pleading to God, for mercy, and for riches,
but his prayers get rejected all the time.
He becomes a zoo animal.
People's stares bite at him.
He does not care.
He dares not taste food from street bins.
He does not know death has surrounded him.

Mother to Daughter
Martin Chrispine Juwa

Even though your face is dim
with the fear of tomorrow,
I will dress you up in meter and rhythm,
to bring enough light in your eyes.
I will plait your hair in similes and metaphors,
I will paint your heart in colours of the prism
just like an old slave woman training her grandchildren
to sing ancient Negro songs.
I will build you up, patiently,
as a stone smith works on crumbled rock.
I will push you up the ladder of acceptance, Emily,
so that you break open
And stretch your wings, oh little caterpillar, and
fly away to a world of rest
because my heart cannot keep you anymore…

Night Dancers
Martin Chrispine Juwa

While in the heavens above
the silver moon hangs serene
in its lustrous beauty.
Men and women
take the warm night in their blood flow
as they float in dance and laughter.

While breeze drifts, and the moon energies the darkness,
little babies' gums cling to their mothers' breasts,
and timid children thread their hands into their fathers' palms;
they shake their heads to the music of the *Malipenga* dancers.

In all this merriment, I want to know him who first danced here
and sung his soul out to the grinning moon.
I want to share a moment with him who first
upon the ocean of twinkling stars dedicated his whistle and drum
to the gods.
I wish to recollect that past when dancers first beheld
their mirrors to the god of light and harvest.
I want to know when the stars and lovers first kissed each other
good night

Malipenga is a local Malawian dance performed by the Yao tribe.

story of a dog
Anton Krueger

(for Zanethemba)

…inja ….zi zinja…inja…

there's a dog that walks the streets
looking for meat, for something to eat,
looking for something to feed on…

…zi zinja yonke dawo…zi zinja…

there's a dog that wants to get out of the cold,
wants a place out the rain, where it can stay and grow old,
wants to grow a few flowers, raise a pup or two,
somewhere near a rubbish dump, away from you…

there's a dog that's scratching at the fleas on its back,
there's a dog that's waiting and its ready to attack,
because … its overthinking… dog wants to defend
wants to be safe, every dog needs a friend…

…kuyo yonke indawo kukho izinja...

doesn't know he doesn't need to scratch,
doesn't know he doesn't need to bite,
doesn't mean to attack, but –

...he's overthinking...

this dog is nobody's pet,
this dog has never seen a vet.
this dog has some barking still to do, this dog,
this dog is running between me and you... ...this dog...

...*zi zinja yonke dawo...zi zinja...*

scratching, biting, barking
– one ear torn, one eye out –
this dog is thirsty, this dog is afraid,
this dog is overthinking,
as I tried to explain...

... *inja ....zi zinja...inja...*

this dog has some barking still to do, this dog,
this dog is running between me and you...

...this dog...

how foil absorbs blood
Richeal Barnes

i was my father's tongue when
he first had me. and his heartache
and his unguarded manhood,
shaped like a suit case handle.
no pride of origin nor belonging.
i knew this from my mother who
learnt from her mother who was
not birthed, but inherited under
the rubbles of men who did not die
but collapsed out of purge. a blue
sleeve caftan, i imagine the tart
taste of grapes in father's upper
pocket and think that love is
a contest of how bad you resist
to rust. one night something
happened; all the women staged
a war against him. in what looked
like a turn by turn cremation of
scars that return by their ashes.
inside the shrine of forgetfulness
they scooped hostile rituals on their
heads; noun-flakes, the debris of
still-birth curses and overripe stars
melting softly into a steel-liquid-lake.
on the glinting surface, i remember
a girl who is a window, yet

always return to herself with
the wrong keys. the reflection
is a proverb, that many lesions
never go away until you
remorsefully welcome them back
into the body in the dialect of
vengeance. a dream that could
only remain a dream. fathers!
how can you imagine a daughter's
breast in your mouth crammed
with incisors of your own skull?

back seat girls
Richeal Barnes

it took me a while to learn to bury men
under water, that they would not germinate
where they are not ploughed. love means
only one thing; a self-infecting sprain in
the trance of bolting out of loneliness.
in other words; imagine angels holding
you from slipping into a stray-pit but at
night invite you into a bigger grave, sit on
its brink and eat your own bones with you.
the sun titters as though everything is
perfect just after the feast, when your
lover's fingers, heavy with aggressive
mint says open your legs; without
understanding why silence is the most
loyal dialect to the soil; why you should
not drown God who is a man in water.
because He who clones gills is a
preamble of survival. i have murdered
all men yet, they keep breaking out
of my mother's water like seasons.

WALKING ON THE RIM OF RAIN
Abubakar A. Yunusa

I have walked the edge of wetness,
where silence writes its name in mud,
where puddles mirror fathers we forgot—
half-rain, half-ghost.

In the market of drowned dreams,
I bought a jar of thunder
and traded it for a dry season.
What is drought but thirst with pride?

I dance barefoot where clouds retire—
the rim of rain holds my name gently.

THE MAP THAT BURNS
Abubakar A. Yunusa

My skin is a map they try to redraw—
colon lines, capital scars,
rivers renamed with conquest.

Each scar tells a journey,
each breath a rebellion.
I am not a country;
I am the scream before borders.

In my chest is a compass—
it only points to ancestors
still hiding in my poems.

TO THE CHILD WHO HID BEHIND TOMORROW
Abubakar A. Yunusa

Little one,
who folded yesterday into a kite
and flew it over grief—

you are not forgotten.

The moon remembers your footprints.
The trees hum your lullaby.
The sky still wears
your unfinished questions
like jewelry made of silence.

Come home,
your name is still valid here.

Le mien
Nellah Nonkondlo Mtanenhlabathi

Like how I bath for a minute and stand for 30 in the shower
just enjoying water hitting my body as hot as it "ease" its soothing
and painful not even I feel nor see my own tears
It's just washed away without a trace.
Only because he is not around.

Together we mess the glass and the tiled walls
Painting them with our palms
Fingers just Tattooing everything
From the back of his head
Down the neck to the spinal code

I love his back
He said he didn't love my hands touching his bunda but it's bigger
than mine and I enjoy playing with it
I hit it like a drum
He stares   I draw him closer to my lips
I caress them again
He pauses   my tongue finds its way to the

ears

My hands are glued until my back is on the walls

My punishment!

My half an hour takes more than that because we are together today
Him scrubbing and kissing my shoulders
I am a baby washed until it's time to dry up
I can't cry or throw myself down, that tantrum, I have not but I clench the balls
His warm lips on my ear
I am ready until he whispers
"We can't stay here forever "

Like how the tub has been his pillow
Listening to his problems
His panics
His shuts
His feeble thoughts, mind
Tired body

Until I join him just sitting on him playing with his nipples
Finger on my clit a minute then the labs …,
I am statured
His future plans; Only thing making sense.
 I am a part of it
Whatever sounds I am making are poisoned with lies
I am not here with him
I am there with him, where he saw us
Only a tongue on my belly button brings me back to life

Whatever happens next is between the tub, my back and everything in the bath house.

You just go to HELL!
Nellah Nonkondlo Mtanenhlabathi

As for you ma'am
I am exasperated by your lack of normality
Such a gobshite klutz!

Between your mother's funeral and gallivanting with your niece
Your choice is whoring
Your CHOICE!
Bad! bad! bad!
So young but old in areas you shouldn't
Who taught you about condoms anyway?
So confident yet very shy for Algebra

If it's not short its nudeness
If it's not listening it's Cursing
If She chooses girls you support her
If it's not an Elder it's your father
If it's not home it's soccer you can't even kick a ball what are you doing there?

Can't you be firm?
Focus on the cumulonimbus and the Mutapa state before "boys because boys brings babies "?
A school Vs a Club
A family Vs a god
A church Vs a game
A sister Vs a whore

Reality Vs stupidity
Good Vs evil
Books Vs ball
Valedictorian Vs tainted achievements
Studying Vs gossiping
Honesty Vs Fallacy and mendacious

You always go for the latter!

You are not spoiled but spoilt
Rotten, Decayed, Decomposed, Contaminated, Putrid, Sour, Polluted, Atrocious!
FOUL!

I would have started my letter with "dear "but you "ain't "that dear to me
Hey uterine sibling (calling you a sibling sounds wrong, STRANGER!
I have no affection whatsoever for you now
I can't bring myself to despise you, you are too much of a horror for me to care
I didn't exhaust much but your ears are solid rock for you to listen
You have no heart and easily swayed or you act like it
I am not pained by your words or actions but your LACK in everything
I don't need to repeat myself again
You picked thorns, allow them to prickle you

I care less about your age or my defensive thoughts about how you do things
As different as we are if I am able to reason at your age why can't you?
It's simple, Use Water, nothing to think hard about there but like your niece you are too stupid for me to argue with, for starters I wouldn't laugh at a person Praying and having a breakdown in their bedroom because I saw them
I wouldn't hook up my brothers with the same girl
Encourage my cousin to pursue my niece again or argue with a motherly figure I only have
Not me then, now or Ever!
The next time you get disciplined avoid changing the narrative you might find yourself sitting on the floor crying, trying to pick a fight with me again
I am still the "Ants that killed an elephant"
My fist is as strong as my nib!
I regretted, sparing the rod to spoiling you to driving foolishness from your heart with that rod of correction to low leg kicks since you thought you're Tong Po unaware I am Van Damme
Beware of a ushiro Geri in your face that will bring you back to reality and choke you to telling the truth that time around! I am not your cup of tea!
For the dignity of family and because I wouldn't finish, I'll stop here
Make amendments with the rents before it's late
I almost left you an address for corrections but that will look like an invitation, stay in your pit!
You are a real definition of puke

Hopefully by the time you get this you will be woke and literate enough for this poem.
I am erasing all the sweet memories ahead I planned for us
Even if you come back to your senses, I would have melted away to entertain you again
Loving you from a distance

That Woman who was born fourteen years before you were!

Dancing with the Devil
Nellah Nonkondlo Mtanenhlabathi

Attached
        Bound
  Loved
        NO!   they pretend!

She said she wouldn't leave her home because her cows will destroy her neighbour's field
But
Said she wouldn't let her sister suffer to me

Lies
    Liar

        Chameleon tongued wretch!

Curses
        Cursed
Rotten heart   Jealousy

Women!
        Yes Mothers!
Wicked
        Night riders
Day lovers
        Just vipers

Blood sucking vampires!

She snapped: "you will lose the house
You will look for me
The other: "they will die poor looking for jobs, not getting any
Chasing paper in a whirlwind
They will look for me

They should tell us their plans!

Oh my daughter
My grandchild

Deaf.

Dumb.

Blind.

Act1: Never get caught,pretend!

Binded
    By
        Blood

                        Separated
                By
          Grace.

For He Knows the plans He has
HIM the I AM not them!

      Saved

I got my dance but the music stopped!

Burning Soil
Innocent Chima Ogoke

I have seen Owerri bleed at midnight,
gunfire stitching fear into the wind.
The streets whisper of stolen sons,
of mothers who light candles that never burn out.

Corruption wears a governor's smile,
his hands thick with the weight of stolen bread.
They build mansions from our hunger,
lace their pockets with our future's bones.

Yet, love still blooms in this ruin,
two hearts meeting under a broken streetlamp,
a promise made where silence listens,
a kiss stolen before sirens wail.

Greed walks these roads in polished shoes,
sipping fine wine as bodies fall.
The city is an open wound,
but my voice will not be buried in its dust.

I will plant words like seeds in scorched earth,
raise walls where hope once crumbled.
A country is not its thieves,
but the hands that dare to rebuild.

Let them burn this soil if they must—

from the ashes, a nation will rise.

Tongues of Reconciliation
Innocent Chima Ogoke

In the valleys where rifles chant,
new tongues must rise—not steel,
but seed. Not revenge,
but the rustle of grain
shared between once-clashing hands.

We have heard the herdsmen's grief
spelled in ash on yam fields.
We have read farmers' anger
in bullet-bored barns.
Even the wind now wails
in borrowed tongues of sorrow.

But let us teach our children
another dialect—
not of loss, but of land healed.
Let prayers be replanted
as community orchards.

Let meetings bloom
where machetes once slept.
Let elders reword grudges
into grazing routes and compromise.

The tongue of tomorrow
must hum in co-ops,
in market pacts,
in schools where tribe
is not a threat but a thread.

And the loudest voice—
for once—must be peace
spoken fluently by all.

PEACE
Ibadin Kingsley

Peace is air
We must need air
Peace is water
We must need water
Peace is blood
We must have blood
In our veins
Peace is our life

Right to life
Right equity, fairness and justice
Right to freedom of worship
They are our inalienable rights

The peace of
The body, spirit and soul
Is the essence of life
Peace is now a cripple
This crippled peace has been murdered

If we say
Peace is life
Then the enemy of peace
Is our common enemy

We must not allow it

We must not allow them

Our shattered limbs
Our dismembered bodies
Our unmarked shallow anonymous graves
Our dispossessed ancestral lands

Our orphans, our widows
Our widowers, our homelessness
Our erased communities

The annihilation! The genocide!
The heinous culture of silence
In the liberalization of evil

Are the evidence
We are the living evidences
So, we know it.

VILLAGE BOY
Agufa Kivuya

Call me the Christian Poet,
Call me the village boy,
Because the city has refused to swallow it,
Just wandering around the meandering way,
Not one seems like the real Way.
Everywhere you stumble upon the garbage,
Always smoking the pollution,
Wary of the sniffing dogs,
Littered all over the highways,
Why are the cities highways complicated?
Always resembling one another,
Confusing the village boy,
Not sure which way is the Way,
Maybe I need spectacles,
No, the cities need to clean up itself,
To draw a white line between the Way and ways.

WHERES THE KING
Agufa Kivuya

Weeping is strewn everywhere,
Some loudly and others silently,
A father turns on the mother with blows,
A son turns against the father,
The fighting goes round and round.
One man rises up,
With a gun swinging on his shoulders,
Not to protect the beleaguered,
But to spray the beloved young ones with bullets,
Maybe unaware of the tears he will elicit,
Filling the whole world with sorrows.
A mother wakes up to bid her daughter goodbye,
Repeatedly reminding her of the need to work hard in school,
Only for the people from another world to emerge,
Without pity, holding other people's daughters hostage,
With impunity spewing threats and ultimatums,
The world clamor and tears helping not.
The night seems over as the light shines at the end of the tunnel,
As the rejoicing over the light picks up,
All over a sudden another night creeps in unannounced,
Because of yesterday's sorrows nobody wants to be part of the today's night,
Where is the much needed light?
The whole world wants the light,
With tears the world calls for the king of Salem,
The prince of peace come back to us,

We need the king of Salem,
The world is in turmoil.

IN THE RACE
Agufa Kivuya

Seated on a sofa
Gazing at the wall
Aware of the ticking sound
I mean rankling ticking noise
Realizing the underestimated speed,
Just yesterday I was crafting
Planning for the year
Broadly smiling at the new year resolutions
Seeing only light
But the year being almost gone
Some resolutions impossible
Others reframed
The ticking noise showing no sign of abating or slowing down
Sometimes a year is too short
Especially when resolutions are splendid
You can run
But never against time
You can compete
But never against a ticking clock
You can listen to various sounds
But not a ticking sound against your estimates.
But God always gives us another year

DREAMSIDE EXCHANGE
Francis Otole

Weaver bird, weaver bird
of the Benue riverbed
sitting high and calm
on a solitary palm.

Tell me what thou see
across this sea?
What is the bond
between here and beyond?

Little child, little child
tender and mild
you enquire
as curiosity require.

Many crossings have shown
what lies beyond is unknown.
I think the smiling water lotus
bear messages of those that left us.

CANONS FOR CANNONS
Francis Otole

For long we have matched
Blood for blood
Bullet for bullet
Teeth for tat
Eye for eye
Yet widening the crack.
Now let's dissolve in order to resolve,
To bridge the differences
By trading canons for cannons
And missals for missiles.

TOWARDS PERFECTION
Francis Otole

Looking down the road
With many going to and fro
Back and forth
Left and right
Up and down
Fast and slow.
When I asked their direction
They said "Towards perfection"

The Noon
Imemba Emmanuel Ikechukwu

A Toad does not run in the daytime in vain— Igbo proverb

When I was created, God said "leap!" and not "run". Leap. That is the first thing I should correct. The second, and the most important, is that I am not only a lover of water; lover because the glassy nature of water throws more light to the very essence of purity. Lover because I do not see the reason why one, who blesses his throat with a great amount of purity, should be referred to as me with a voice that wears exasperation.

So yes, I am not only a lover of water, but also of grass; how its soft tips harbors the tiny droplets of the morning dew. How much it retains its moist, holding firm to the little portion of purity that it was given. Of children; how they bask in awe when they get a glimpse of me, resting amidst the grasses. How they squeak— those tiny voices that mirrors the world's innocence.

And lastly, the noon— and that is where you get it all wrong. How could one live and not love the noon?; the sun glistening high above with its heavenly glory, the Morning glory spreading its hands to the warm embrace of sunlight. In vain? When the beaches are filled with happy people, the waters reaching out to the lovers, to the newly wedded couples, to the single mother and her baby, caressing their legs, and they laugh to this bliss the noon has given them.

What other time is best for spectating?. Tell me, what other blessing supersedes the brightness of this period, when all the universe is alive and beautiful?

Do not label me a murderer of trees
Imemba Emmanuel Ikechukwu

A river does not flow through the forest without bringing down trees —
Proverb .

There is me,
Who was there when the universe was yet blind.
Me, who sheltered the earth before the first breaking of silence;
before God decided to let her see;
before she decided to be a mother—
she said, *reach out and make me a woman,*
and God, in all his benevolence, impregnated her with seeds.

I was there at the divine consummation.
 It was me, who protected those babies from the dryness of their mother's womb.
Those children, who have grown to recycle the very air that feeds your lungs.
Who now serve as nests to the singing nightingale and the squawking kites.
Do you not see the Yankari warm spring, the Ụbakala waterfall?
How I've continued to stretch my arms and legs,
how I've become a father who keeps their throat away from threatening dryness.

Then, there's you,
Who cuts her children till they split and die,

till their sap spills over like congealed blood.
You slit their throat as if you've never licked a mango from their bosom,
as if your nose doesn't munch on the clean air they cycle,
as if dogoyaro do not cure your malaria,
as if they do not preserve you.

See the ail of grief you inflict on her—
her grief extends into a deep hole in her heart—
See how you call it erosion.
She weeps:
Now her wrath descends like the plague of Egypt—
the air is poisonous,
the insects have moved on,
famine, drought — now she rejects me, the constant source of her initial wetness—
She holds onto death with vengeance in her mouth,
and in consolation I've asked her, the definition of death for one who could never die.

So do not label me a murderer of trees.
Do not accuse me for the sins of your sap hungry axes,
for at each fall of those children that I nurtured from the beginning, I weep.
At each unpleasantness of their mother's wailings, I weep.
And I know, that you, in all your brilliance, can never picture the very image of a water's tears,
and that is the ground, for which your accusations have been laid.

Let them eat what they serve others
Obinna Chilekezi

*"hate, it has caused a lot of problems
in the world but it has not solved one yet"*
Maya Angelou

Ephemeral
Fleeting foot of peace of the day
We can't be tired of the mundane
From sad dull moments
Of the day with dull excitement
And of hate bliss, raising up arms
Crippling about the day in shambles

It leaves behind door anger and sorrow
As sorrow filled the land like hurricane
It steals our joy, our enthusiasm, our lives
Jaded we become, after years of same sorrow
Same sadness

Mae culpa!
What a mistake, yes wrong ones on throne
And ours the killing cry, death and hunger
Give us peace we plead to stony eardrums
Give us peace our hearts whispered loudly
A cosy, comfortable feeling of peace and love
We dream of, in a world so full of crises

That's hygge!

We wish them those in power that they serve us
Tears, sorrow and wants! Serve the offspring same as they serve
Let them steal from our wants crisis of life.
We are tired of their schadenfreude, yes we are tired of wants
In this land of plenty. Let them eat that they cook for others.

BULLETIN BUGS
Ekundayo Asifat

A punch in the lull
The air turns sombre
A touch sinister
A sullen descent of tumult on the household
Bulletins are the bugs
Devouring fragile hours
The bugs ring loud
A whiff of buzzing about ears
The world repletes
With cries of violence:
Mayhem in Cote d'Ivoire
Liberia shudders in gloom
Nigeria is riddled with crises
Crises of oil and politics
Pakistan bleeds
China shrinks
Yet the cries reverberate
With wars and spate of deaths
Orphans wailings rip shutters
A strange world it turns

The wild horses run wilder
The storm mounts ears
The wireless in endless chattering coughs, hisses and talks:
Our universe shouts hoarse
Earth sinks below hurrying feet

Behold hands are keen on triggers
When men become bloody
And kin deny their own

From the cries, pains and rage of wars
The world pines but seeks restitution
Starvation is the monster
With arms outstretched
Where the land is sacked
And men fleeing from the earth
Bound by wars and storms.

IYA GBOGBO (My step mother)
Ekundayo Asifat

Memories haunt me
 Of the times Iya gbogbo was the pestle
That pounded yam in the mortar
For a house-hold.

Pain was the foe she met
 And strove to tame,
A lean limb That moulded earth into breaths
Tall spirits that built tracks in the world

A land grubber,
She toiled from dawn till dusk
Calmness was her acolytes,
The air, earth and the woods
In mute companionship
 Swerved her thoughts,
Her clothes sprouted holes
 A horde of flies pestered her tools
 Feet smarted from the bite of stones
The dawn set her on journeys
Journeys of slog
Night led her back a dumb lamb
Her room, an ant's hiding.

A pile of cow dung paste
Reeked with remnants of forage

Death came prowling one dusk
 Seized her breath

And cast a void in the home,
Earth, witness

How her sweat probed your entrails
 But termites devoured her harvests.

This is Our Homeland Too
Tlotlisang David Mhlambiso

Oceans and lakes wouldn't have let us float till here,
Ships would have wrecked in the middle of the ocean,
All of us could have drowned even before the dawn,
The sun could have set for us even before the sunset,
But nature has let some float and arrive alive,
While some unwarrantedly flew and landed here,
So safely and healthy with no bite nor scratch,
We indeed belong to this land, our homeland too.
Oh, Dear-born and bred residents, we are your people,
We are black in colour and red in blood, my lineage.
Let peace and love reign freely in these streets,
War ain' t for us; I declare, I am not a refugee,
And so, you, be not xenophobic; indeed, I command,
Because we are all Africans, we are all humans.

Exile me!
Tlotlisang David Mhlambiso

To the streets of no guns and bombs,
Africa! Africa! I can't breathe, exile me!
Axe me out of this continent! Exile me!
For so many riots and protests have caused me
pain, and shattered my hearing buds.

I have lost my Africanity; I say,
I need peace, and in this land, there isn't.
I am eager to hear the birds sing sweet melodies.
And chanting for a beautiful day ahead.
I need to see the sunrise clearly
with no smoke of a burnt tyre on the streets,
And walk on the untrampled dew of the morning.

On the day of my banishment, I will be happy,
For being a refugee will earn me rights in Egypt,
I will belong to their streets; I will be their own,
They shall rejoice at my arrival and give me land.
I will therefore wake up to no wars and riots,
Peace and harmony shall be part of my life!
Oh! The clear sky with no clouds, I see you!

Exile me, Africa! Mercilessly do, I shall rejoice!

If I Make It Back Home
Tlotlisang David Mhlambiso

Call the neighbours,
Brew "mnqombothi",
Slaughter white goat,
Burn incense,
And tell the forefathers
the prodigal son is back.

Sing praises and ululate,
Dance until you can't anymore,
Cry and be loud unashamedly,
For I have survived;

The anger of my kinsmen
in African countries to African men,
The brutality of their guns and
blazing fire up my cottage roof,
Thrown on the streets and
beaten to bruises and scratches
and denied healthcare.

Nevertheless, bury the hatchet,
do good unto them,
they are Africans, my men.

Glossary
Umqombothi - South African homemade traditional beer

Fresh Tears
Wafula Khisa

I see people run from streets
Holding their heads, dodging bullets and irritating gas
Police after them with batons, eager to crush for a hefty reward
And I wonder, what happened here?
Wasn't it the other day, they danced in these streets, carrying
placards and chanting slogans
Celebrating the newcomer, who scattered promises like grains to
starving chickens
And made them lick the honey
That dripped from his deceptive tongue for the kingdom had
come?

I see them wearing sufurias on their heads
Like helmets while singing songs of agony
Plucking wild fruits on streets and tearing our heritage to appease
The demons of anger, digging claws down their dry throats
And I wonder, what happened here?

Didn't they promise to lower branches of the great tree
For hustlers to pick their share of grapes?
Didn't they promise to make the ground easy and even
For hustlers to tread and trade without fear?
Why are they unleashing dragons of taxes to tear us?

What happened to our dreams of a better day?
Did they grow wings and fly away like a distressed bird?

When the shepherd mutated into a blood-sucking hound
Turned against the flock, scattered and subdued it
And put its precious life at risk?
What happened to faces that glittered and glowed
When victory smiled ahead and we ran to embrace it?
If we had known our smiles would fade away like dew at dawn
And sunrise bring fresh tears to sting our eyes at daybreak
We'd have embraced pain; nothing good happens here!

Reign of Terror
Wafula Khisa

Go tell our people
To brace for a rough ride and deadly crash
Brakes have failed and driver turned rogue
Here comes taxman, with big knife and roaring appetite
To mutilate starving payslips, fuel, laughter and breath--
everything!
And nobody protests, unless you love this country more than life
Here comes uniformed men, eager to shoot and kill
For badges of honour from commander.

Six went down today
Others dance in streets, waiting for angels of darkness
To come down and carry them away on lethal wings
They nurse bullet wounds after a bloody and noisy bath
That left these streets dressed in an ugly mess
And our laughters swallowed by gunshots and sirens.

They pounced on Owino this morning
Roughed him up and dragged him around town
Starved him for days and pinched him to accept the new god
When they finally arraigned him, his spirit was down
He had to submit to their biting arrogance and tyranny
To stay alive and go home.

They invaded our homes like uninvited guests
Sprayed them with gas and made us run to their biting arms
For deadly embrace of batons, bullets and water canons
They chase us from streets to silence us at home
Must we fall for them to remain standing?

To stay alive here, one must be ready to die
Hide your face in sand when a friend is strangled next door
Shut your mouth when robbed, and speak not
Fill your ears with cotton, ignore children's cry of hunger
Because nobody tells a king he's naked!

You're Not the Friend I Knew
Wafula Khisa

Today you disappointed me again, friend
You called me ugly names and threw mud at me
You buried your head in sand & left your men crucify me for badges of honour
You enjoyed the comfort of a warm bed as rain and cold kept my sleep at bay
You smiled over a sumptuous meal as I ate tear gas and dust in streets
Chanting our newfound slogans and freedom songs
That deny you peace and appetite.

Today you broke my heart again, mate
Stripped me naked, crushed my bones and spilled my blood
Painted streets red and scared everyone from asking the right questions
Like why rising from the bottom remains a nightmare to everyone
And why this country hurts everywhere, even after milking us dry
Today you ordered noisemakers & busybodies to lose legs
and stay home to watch you make great speeches & promises
Is it because we're tired of mourning
or not everyone has to disappear?

You stopped being my friend, when you wore the crown
and turned your back on the little things that bound us.
What evil thing entered your DNA?

What speck blinded your eyes?
Who stuffed cotton in your ears?
Do you ever listen to night songs, cries of agony &
countless petitions the wind carries to your doorstep?
If you label everyone that points fingers at you as tribal, an evil to
be terminated
Honestly, I don't understand you anymore.

If you must eat the game we hunted together
Let's breathe, walk & live
To watch you enjoy the party with friends.

HER LOST LOVER
Ngcali Angelica Xhegwana

I found her lying among a bed
of dwindling roses; a sign
of their dying love. I found her
crying, while curled on their

matrimonial bed; holding on
to the love letters he gave her
when she was 16, Crying as she
stared softly at the rotten

bouquet besides her bed-frame.
She'd hate to see him in a bad-frame.
Even through her swollen eyes;
Broken promises...broken limbs...

Which ones better?
She fluttered her eyes, trembling...as she
held on to the tattered teddy bear, with a
golden heart on it written "I'm sorry". She

smiled (softly), even as the movement hurt
her to breathe; Even as she re-cushioned
herself to make haste of the pain...

2/4

She couldn't hold back her tears as she
stared at a lone red rose, out of the many
rotten petals; out of the many rotten
memories. She lightly sobbed,

unable to hold herself back;
Red roses; dwindling fires... her heart
ached; unable to breathe properly she held
on to her aching chest... The teddy bear

left unravelled as it tumbled
out of her hands... Out of her hold.
The love letters rippled with the
winds as they danced with the

pure white curtains, which with
their movements brought an
encasing of light with them.
She lay there, on their matrimonial

bed, curled in the fatal position...
playing with the diamond studded
promise ring he got her on
their 5th year anniversary...encased

by the diluted smell of dying roses...and a
glimpse of red, beneath them red...red
which bled from her. She hastily grabbed
the lone live flower, twirling it around her

ring finger; Red...almost as red as this.
"Green..." she whispered softly,
stroking the green of the leaves
on the stem of the sturdy rose...that

was how healthy their relationship started.
Like plants on great soil;

3/4

She gripped it softly in her hand, her hold
on it tightening as the seconds passed.
The light from the dancing, twirling
curtains, which with them brought an
encasing of light,

Light which seeped into her concentrated,
tired eyes; Almost ethereally as she stared
enarmoured with the rose;
The last remaining piece of their love.

She gripped it harshly, as if the bitter
memories swallowed her whole and left
her feeling intoxicated. The thorns

of the beautiful rose bit into her

soft, supple skin...
Red roses on crimson painted skin...
She stared dazedly {transfixed} at the
sight...

Just as she could barely register the click
of a click of a door, and the shuffle of the
shoes she bought for him after a
successful job interview; she blinked

softly (weakly, in panicked motions),
in rapid motions, As for dying comfort.
 She absently reached for the teddy
bear, tainting it with her bloodied
fingers

4/4

She hugged the teddy bear close to her, as
the rose invertedly dug closer to her
heart... the thorns now becoming daggers,
she gasped, sobbing

The bed now a pool of bloodied roses, and
her, a dwindling flower; arching as it
reached for its last rays of sunshine.
"Hello lover!" his bright smile was the last
image, she saw. Still sobbing,

she stared at him, smiling,
(back at him) through the pain,
through the loss she already felt...
The guilt consumed her numbing

brain, Her body could barely move,
she conceded. As she could hardly
blink her eyes, she could barely
register the frown tugging on

his eyes, his mesh briefcase
hardly making a sound as it
dropped to the floor, tears
flowing down his face like majestic

waterfalls of some far-away
island. Probably where he would
 be, a month from now... with her
[slung by his shoulders]

"Goodbye, lover' was all she
could manage before she joined
the rotten flowers besides her.

The Wilderness
Janet Patricia Chikoja

Masquerading itself as life!
What is it made of?
A river that rejuvenates my soul?
Or maybe a forest of ideas
From whence hails a hurricane
That sucks dry the very essence of life?
Maybe it is just stones that I take for gran~~ite grant~~ed; or
Thorns and thickets that fringe around the labyrinth of life,
A labyrinth paraded in storms.

Sometimes:
I meander, drift and glide in the storm.
I wonder and wander in the wilderness.
I lose myself in its labyrinth.
I trip, fall and reap bruises from its granite stones.
I disperse ideas by burning the forest with anger.
I fail to read between the line:
'This is just a wilderness parading in front of me as existence'.

Zomba Mountain
Janet Patricia Chikoja

You are majestic, Zomba Mt.
A willowed thicket of glory
A canopy of a World of Forms.
When the wit wades through your shining whispering stream,
The swish of your river
Sings to the soul and tranquillizes the spirit.

The granites that squat before you, Zomba Mt
Re-fashion images of Napolo in the mind
As your silence rolls the spirit into the world beyond
To retrieve memories of the furious serpent
That wiped away the innocent ancestors
On creating this flamboyance that hedges memoirs of tragedy.

Bamboos, mahoganies and creepers
Weave together in bonded relationships.
Your swift-running Mulunguzi stream
Whispers swift, sweet melodies to the spirit
Fueling the soul's mayhem to flutter and dance in the stream's breeze
As it flows down to Zomba city
Whose fierce fire consumes the harmony in nature.

As your rivulet flows down to the city,
The silent voice rolls the spirit high up the mountain.
Oh! Zomba Mt, the forest of romance and memories

The swish of your stream
Siphons the cacophony of human angst.

CAUTION
Janet Patricia Chikoja

When life is a towering height
That looks glorious from Beneath
The lizard comes from Benevolent One
Hugging a message of death
And plunges life into a bottomless pit.

We are flowers
Sprouting in the middle of the night
Blossoming in the morning dew
Flourishing at noon
Withering and falling into the abyss at sunset.

Waiting for the Sun
Yvonnie S. Kunkeyani (Just Sam)

In this dim lit room
I dream...

Of amber specks of your light,
Will they seep into these walls?
Pass those cracks?
Pass through these cracks in my heart?

Your gentle touch...
I will rise,
When you rise.

Of old habits that die hard
Yvonnie S. Kunkeyani (Just Sam)

Of old habits that die hard
I write.
I write poems into our silence.

I imagine you laugh
You sound like music.
I laugh
I write
I write how I am happiest with you beside me.

I remember how you feel,
You feel like home.
I smile
I write
I write about warmth and comfort in your arms.

I should stop.
You are not mine.

Her Nine Lives
Yvonnie S. Kunkeyani (Just Sam)

There is an old saying;
"A cat has nine lives.
For three he plays,
for three he strays,
and for the last three he stays."

Or you can just drown it with:
hands,
pressure,
fear,
and no consent.

With her nine lives,
she has been drowning,
slowly...

This will be our little secret

your mother will never believe you

Don't you dare scream

Show me how much you love me

Then why are you here if not for that?

you asked for it

you are not trying hard enough, are you sure you want the promotion?

It's my bloody husband right, don't make me feel bad.

I am here for the cleansing ritual...

All her life,
Slowly drowning...

The Museum
Kirsten Miller

(For Sibusiso Mthembu)

Who gave it to them, you said.
Who folded up the skins of animals
Into whose eyes you looked,
Wrapped them in a Checkers bag
And asked, What can I get for this lot?
Who gave them the stars
And the moons of millennia
Caught in clay pots, and told us:
We have no need for this now.

Who took the birds from the sky
And the footprints of princes
And brought these to the steps
Of the museum?
Who forgot their land and their longing
Secured their positions and tenders
Put their children in the schools
of the oppressors, across the sea?

Who called our culture obsolete,
Climbed into the suburbs
And closed the gates?
What heritage do we have now,

You said. What heartland,
And what heart?
Who gave them my birthright
And my belongings, you said,
And sold it all for sand?

Building walls
Kirsten Miller

Art is my antidote
to your misogyny,
to the click of the switch,
the swipe of a screen,
the drug
of our daily addictions.
Music is my defence
against your pseudo-feminism,
the catch in your
voice that betrays each man
you claim to have loved.
Beauty is my resonance
against your racism,
the diamond glint
in the corrugated dwellings
and the jewels in the eyes
of those you oppress.

Literature is my heart's song,
I build it as protection
between us, words of longing
and of love, over which
your cynicism can never climb.
Art is my wall
against the state of the nation,

the narcism of the soul.
With beauty and words
I will build these barriers,
protect this territory:
This, here, is my land.

Ask the Sea
Kirsten Miller

Loss is a round hole,
the edges hewn smooth
to make it easier
for things to fall in.
We cannot touch the bottom,
you reach in to find
that little spirit,
your fingers barely skim
the depths of me.

Today it is our dog,
tomorrow our mother
or someone's marriage.
I fish with a line
that extends down
from my eyes,
without bait or a lure.
I can catch, in that brine,
Not a single one of us:

I can only ask the sea.

KING MAKERS
Lungisile Goodwell Mselana

The sun bids goodbye to the mountains
Birds leave their trees and their songs
disappear
Shadows are stepping closer
The night marches faster.

Something will disrupt this flowing peace
of quiet night
I look closer than I should have,
Now I wish such images could be
untied
From the claws of memory.

A gun and a knife are king makers
With eyes closed permanently
I can hear the moans of friends
Uncontrollable bleeding
Tell me I'm dreaming
Around guns are coughing blood.
The lifeless body of the one so young.

The pain says cry
The mind says cry not
Here to raise a voice is death
Here to quiet is the solution.

SCRUPULOUS CAVES
Lungisile Goodwell Mselana

In shadows of darkness
Where doors are locked
A quiet voice in cold distance,
Shouts and wait in vain,
For a promise scribbled on water
Loud in desire -to see the sun,
Behind these concrete walls

I have become a walking eagle,
Scratching the layers of
an emptied surface
Avenues of communication closed
Here;
I am counting my many mortifications
In a quiet battle
A confidence cannot
Breathe in these scrupulous caves.

RELENTLESS DEMONS
Lungisile Goodwell Mselana

In fields of darkness
lies the murderer of the soul
Jealous splits our circle of friends
dwarfs the soul
The rottenness of the bones
Like a demon it does not sit down.

The vulture who relinquishes
our innermost core
It insulates one from people
It destroys the core of humanity

Why are families broken?
Why are churches empty?
Why do we kill each other?

Jealousy erodes
the soil of the soul
Citizens of the island of
selfishness
The boomerang like weapon
Which hurts the attacker
more that the attacked.

Makanai's Rest
Ewurama Tawiah Welbeck

The night before Makanai's body kissed her soul goodbye,
Mama visited her chamber.
She wore a white garb to initiate
Her afflicted soul into wonderland.

I stood bewildered.
Why was mum celebrating her turmoil?
Her body and spirit were enwrapped in ire.
Makanai's soul was disconcerted.
A ruckus erupted from her moans of pain.
Her soul was veiled in torment as
Shades of transition leapt for her.

Incantations dashed out.
Declarations poured out.
Invocations pleaded on.
Yet she refused transition.

I watched with glassy eyes,
As she sang and danced to mama's pleas.
Offense drummed vengeance on her death bed.
She sought the hands that dug her grave.

For heavens were disturbed—
A soul of fire wanted to see God.
She coveted her maker's calm.

So God came out in the cool of His splendor.
He fetched her tears into nature's goblet.

Makanai fell into her box,
As God laid her to rest.

The Sound of Rain
Ewurama Tawiah Welbeck

Thrumming rains dilute the earth's cancer.
It dances along the valleys coaxing forth the soil's ambrosia.
Golden yields of joy welcome us with pelting falls.
Passion(fruits) climb on twining vines as
Cherries redden their fruits dangling on frayed boughs.
Chiuta sprinkles petrichor on earth's sheet
Soothing our lost memories.
Showers of quietude rinse our stained teeth as
Healing pours down mercifully —
Washing our ills in earth's bosom.
On some nights it would drown our lacrimation,
As falling mist settle on our linens.
The rain seeps into our eyes mind
Revealing earth's rejuvenation of harvest.
I see it washing pain ashore,
And hurrying in with glistening drops of hope.
It glories with tiny beats on our hearts
As we merry in its coolness.

The Return of Peace
Ewurama Tawiah Welbeck

The winebiber has fallen into our dragnet.
His blacken soul is convulsing.
He scratches his hanging manhood
Even in his ignominy.
The busy bodies scramble there
To mock and clap hands.
They throw dust around singing tunes
Of ominous verdict.

People are saying
The tattler has been found.
Broken teeth and splinted jaws
Accompany her. She cradles her torn lips
And still gossips in her infamy.
The gawkers scorn at her folly,
Taunting silence out of her misery.

I now say,
Those scoundrels have met their fate
And peace does us the honours of reigning again.

GLOBAL HARMONY
Maryam Shitu Abdulkadir

Like a hollow
Emptiness is found
In this so-called home.

Devoid of good will
Like a man
Mortal is morality

In-existent is property
No personality what's family
How do we stand erect
No freedom nor
World unity?

Future one stepping on stones
Within this unharmonious
Presupposed powerful wealth.

To the your highness
With their dominion
Over the world.

Then, not
Now dear occurring
How do you define this
Empty vessel?

For all it acknowledges
Is the glugging
Of the inhumane.

Does any provision need to be spelt out
......according to
    Pursuant to
Uh-Uh
It's a forgone conclusion
That state of calm
That's life's balm!

RECIPROCITY
Maryam Shitu Abdulkadir

They say
A long-term increase
In the earth's average temperature

But what's more than over said
Is a long-term increase
In the earth's habitats
Conventional-strange departure

A promise and a demise
In between a missile
We are the target of our very own strategy
The cause?
Anthropogenic

To the uncle that
Makes his way to Lagos
The little boy aspiring
To be an engineer
that circle around furnace
And to the blue collar worker
You destroy you

Dear earth's habitats
You're in a flood of destruction
And in a quake of disaster.

ART-AURAL
Maryam Shitu Abdulkadir

Breath
Human origins
Dark skin that shines over the heart

Boasts
Of ancient history
Greatly sophisticated empires

Innumerable
Home to a multitude of cultures
The rainbow in the sky

Beak
Of customs spelt out
In this land
A root in soil

A belief at heart
Rich with rituals
Serene in ceremony
What an art spoken
An art, aural.

SILENT CRY
Comfort Adjeiwaa

Look at you
Trying so hard
Look at you overthinking everything
Look at you
Having an emotional breakdown
Look at you
Faking that great day vibes
When you're burning up inside
No smoke
Just broke

Look at you with that strong faith tower
Sapped energy
Drains
A future with gains
Built from pain
Maybe just a little help would do.

But the reflection hits hard
Cracks unveiling
Hypocrites all around
But with a tiger's observant eye you watch.
Brimming like hot tea vapor.

A silent cry

In the mind's eye
I picture greens
Scenes of freedom.

MASKED
Comfort Adjeiwaa

A fake painting of a smile
A placard with inscription of powerful words
However, a critical look opens up the covered secrets of the human heart

We wear masks to hide our pain,
Conforming to expectations, suppressing our true selves in vain.
The office mask, the social mask, the perfect facade,
But beneath the surface, our hearts are breaking, our souls are frayed.

Silenced, shut down, and forced to comply,
Our emotions buried deep, our true feelings denied.
We're told to be strong, to put on a brave face,
But the weight of our secrets is crushing, a heavy heart's dark place.

If only we could be heard, if only we could speak,
Our hearts might be lighter, our burdens might weaken.
But nobody listens, nobody wants to hear,
Our cries for help, our whispers of fear.

We're lost in a world of expectations, of norms and of rules,
Where authenticity is sacrificed, and true selves are fools.
We're searching for connection, for empathy and understanding,
But it's hard to find, when we're hiding behind masks, pretending.

WHISPERS OF ECHOES
Comfort Adjeiwaa

Silent, soft and quiet
The tendency of an echo to reminisce remnants of the past

Lingering faint memories in the mind
Memories full of subtle voices and intuition that often guide and offer insight
Echoes of the past

Triggered by just a song, a photograph, a scent
Just the slightest thing with access
We time travel for a visit into the past

These echoes whisper secrets which often remind us of our pain, loss, happy, sad, and moment of love
Cherished secrets of the past
Like ripples on our pond, these experiences create concentric circles of memories
Each resonating within the whispers of what has happened before

A bittersweet experience
A reminder of what we lost and gained also
Each whisper echoing sounds like a breeze or loud sounds that threatens to consume us with it's deafening noise.

Even when the night is still,
These whispers echoes can be the loudest

It is in that phase, we are confronted with the emotions we tried to suppress and memories we tried to forget

It is in these moments we learn a lot
We learn to obey the little urge within us
Those little warnings we ignore
We learn to heed to or hearts whisper,
And we find solace in their words.

For in the end the whispers of echoes remind us that we are not alone
We are all a testament to human experience
A tapestry of love, sadness and longing that binds us together

So listen to its gentle voice
Through trails and triumph
For in their soft whispers,
We may discover the secrets of our hearts.

WHEN BOYI WAS ASKED TO DEFINE LOVE...
Alfred Inkah Kamwendo

When Boyi was asked to define love
He searched for the definition in the air
Listened to beehives but found none there
So boyi stopped the search mission
He just set his heart on fire
And found a heated definition
When his eyes kissed Puna's pair of galaxies

Dear ABITI MULI
Alfred Inkah Kamwendo

This spirit found its body in your poetic *padangokhalas*
This body found its soul in your tormenting touch
This soul found its dwelling place in your eager ear
When life was all and it made sense
When dreams were tall and they birthed tense.
This abandoned soul is a morning to regret
This bitter spirit is a longing to let these sinful eyes water
This deserted body is a story to remember
That love was once a living thing, perhaps a cactus
Before love left for *Nsakhuta*—with hope
that you are resting in peace

*padangokhala means folktales
*nsakhuta means graveyard

IN MEMORIAM
Alfred Inkah Kamwendo

Birthed within seconds of ecstasy
When uprooting the sun like a seed seemed a lazy man's task
You didn't ask to be birthed but
The flames of our hearts prayed for days like December 31st
Some joined sinners in abusing trees; jotted you down on papers
Some joined saints in serving trees; jotted you in their troubled minds
Pregnant with hope that when a seed is sown, a plant germinates
And the cycle keeps on going and going and growing
Six moons down the line, you are being sown
Not as a seed that speaks of germination
But as a dead Chitedze root that must be forgotten forever

You were not only goals,
You were the conduit of purpose, perhaps
until we meet again on December 31st

Regards,
A successful failure

Allegories
Ismail Bala

i.   A Tale

There was a boy who left with a wolf
on a winding path. He'd never before stepped beyond the gate

but she came to him with her hollow howl
and he let the kettle boil dry on the stove,

the books still open on the table, left his painted
toys and the unfinished hum of wonder

to follow her through ravines, through groves of wild tafasa.
They wandered beneath bent branches and slept

under stars, on fallen needles. They wandered
and wandered, and in the end that's what remained,

they weren't prophets, they couldn't read
each other's minds. Through the ribs and tunnels

of their open hearts moved their quiet aches,
and nowhere on the earth could they put them down,

they adored the world too deeply: the smoke
and dark rivers, the startled deer.

ii A Myth

There was a woman who ran with a hawk
beyond the orchard fence. She'd never once broken the horizon

but he circled down with fire in his wings
and she left the soup cooling on the wooden stove,

the beds unmade in the yellow house, left her quiet
books and the unfinished thread of longing

to chase him over dunes, through fields of unfurling cotton.
They passed under open skies and rested

in dust, among reeds. They wandered
and wandered, and in the end that was all they knew—

they weren't saints or monsters, they couldn't speak
the language of each other's dreams. Through the fibres and veins

of their bare bodies ran the hush of old griefs,
and nowhere in the turning world could they set them free—

they were too taken by the flame: the cliffs
and moonlit ponds, the startled hares.

Offering
Ismail Bala

It rests on his thigh, quiet, asleep
in the hush between them. She leans in,
lips brushing, a kiss like dusk on still water.
She cradles him, gentle,
as if shaping warmth from clay.
He sighs. Not from need,
but from knowing.

She draws him in, slowly,
and breath awakens him.
He stirs beneath the tide,
grows in her mouth's soft hush.
She's patient—pulling him back from the edge
like a lover gathering
a falling star.
He'll hold her close
when morning comes.

She traces him, fingers delicate,
finding life in the shell
that holds his ache.
She's all around him now,
two hands, third wave,
and when he spills
it's not just release—

but devotion, the shimmer
of something shared.
She gathers it with grace,
tongue a ribbon,
kisses the quiet
returning to him.

He thinks it's over.
But she is still with him.
She opens her satchel,
unwraps a silk length, a silver thread,
and a vessel made for breath,
for rhythm, for something more.

And Then Now
Ismail Bala

(for Carol Ann Duffy)

Then with their hands they would light flame
clutch cup tap glass frame

Then with their weary hands rest
on a bench, leaning their chest

Then with warm hands clasp other palms
or trace soft skin in nighttime calms

Then with their hands on the stone
they would mourn, quiet, alone.

DOWNTOWN HARARE
Simbarashe Nyatsanza

Nose bleeding headache blood
as the bus finally reaches
the city.

Stepping out to hawkers hawking
wares into the headache ear
 - bananas, cable chargers, rat poison,
winter hats, aphrodisiacs,
bring-back-lost-lover medicine, screwdrivers,
shoe polish, cancer cures,
toothpaste, cigarettes, mirrors,
airtime,
second hand underwear.

Night-skinned blood-eyed street touts
bodies limp and warped into
deflated deadening shapes of desparation
caricatures of decency,
cry out to carry the luggage
scanning among passengers for their
next meal
their next hit
their next ride on the wings of backroom made
euphoria
to the blacked-out
indifferent comforts of

syringed oblivion.

The police with batons
screaming sirens
chasing after the unlicensed kombis,
smashing unlicensed window screens,
glass smithereens
on the council tar
- the people's tar -
running after the city rugrats,
- grandmothers manning vegetables outside supermarkets,
blind beggars preaching salvation,
leg-bent cripples singing heart wrenching mercy jingles -
beating them up,
with a smell for the people's blood
in their nose,
like uniformed reapers.

The downtown rundown Sunshine City
smelling of hard urine
corridors littered by used condoms
children of the streets gazing,
calculating
whose pockets contain today's meal
shops bossed by Somalis, Nigerians, Congolese,
while
the sons of the soil keep
wailing the childhood learned
generational refrain

"the country is hard, so hard,
harder than an
adolescent erection".

Piss stained walls smelling,
posters with the ruling face,
disappear into the smoke
as far as the eyes are willing
to see.

Ghetto graffiti echo slogans of
resistance,
of the blood of all those heroes
despondently reeking of
burst sewage pipes that give the capital
city its pauper's scent.

And at the roundabout a
30 tonne lithium hauling truck
- China bound -
falls over
a 17 sitted kombi like an iron
ironing ghetto dreams and ghetto lives and ghetto loves
and ghetto journeys,
flattening everything
until the blood curling
screams from inside the mangled
carcass of a kombi
finally stop

and the blood
flows
- like that of the people's heroes -
into the sewage pool
next to the okra vendor.

Harare with bulging blood stained
eyes dreaming while awake,
never sleeping, never relenting
wheezing, waiting, watching,
like the Malawian hijabi
selling her pork pies right at the
church entrance.

THE CONFIRMATION OF ROT
Simbarashe Nyatsanza

Buttocks sweat-stuck next to each other
in the Honda Fit.
The underarm is a battle of rotting
middle-class zhing-zhong scents.
In the eight passengered five-sitter
that left no room for dignity.
The wife the sister and I
squeezed inside a single coffined seat.
The perfect ride.

Outside the window pane
the rotund, bulbous rock meandering
mountains of Boterekwa,
now Chinese-excavated,
scarred at the sides,
fester minerals - chrysotile, lepidolite,
cesium, tantalum - like a pus-lubricated maggot-infested wound
into the ever gulping mouth that is the
Scania,
Some kind of unsatiable vagina.

And then finally the destination.
The perspicacious Madzibaba is sun sitted
underneath a sprawling skeletal msasa tree.
Starlink perched on the roof
of a child drawn fowl run

like some strange crown of absurdity.
Then he changes into his mud stained gemenzi,
the appropriate apparel
for reading our obfuscated and futile futures
while his microcephalised son
 - his eyes bulging out of his face like a rubber doll squeezed
 - runs to the kitchen to
fetch water for his father's thirsty
out of town guests.

Then one by one, we truckled our worth before him
at the claypot and chicken-feather adorned shrine,
like the digits of a fisted hand - folded
to the core.
He gives each the deleterious fate
each had came to so preciously confirm;
the family killer curse is coming
for everyone because the early fathers
violated resting bodies - for power.
And sent undeserving souls to an undeserving purgatory.
And now it's coming.
For everyone.
One. By. One.

The prospect wife I'd been nidificating with
nuddles her way back to my numbified arms,
meacocked by her presented fate
of carrying babies that keep dying because
they're fathered by a cursed lineage.

The loquasious sister remains
kneeling before him seeking clarity
talking of dreams and night sweats and voices of deadmen
that she keeps hearing.
And I?
I am recalcitrant no more.
I am Christ on the cross.
I am requiescence.

Madzibaba prescribes more gift carried shrine visits,
and smooth prayer flavoured pebbles
to drink and to wash ourselves with
in order to wade off the spirits of
vengeance
and the wrath of the angry ancestors.

The now gaunt hollowed-in,
deflated rock mountains
sneer sullen smiles of mockery
past the window pane,
like devil-sent ghouls
of dreamland trolls.

POETS DON'T GET PAID HERE
Simbarashe Nyatsanza

The job isn't jobbing properly.
Hours and hours of peg searching
demarcating suburbs that the rich
will live and continue to be rich in.
Supervising the casual labour
from the village
digging trenches to draw water
from the 4-1 Brigade to the low density suburbs.
Developing the land
 - our land.

The office lady says the money isn't in yet.
Head office is facing a backlog
And some of us
have only been employed out of pity.
Remember that, she says.

Days have been cut off from the week.
Tomorrow and the next and the next day
noone should come in because
noone will get anything.
There will be no money.

Then later in the afternoon
at the publisher's office
the editor's response acquiescences

that the poems dropped earlier
are too wound up and rigid and personal
and therefore
couldn't be published here.

They need to be tweaked a little beat.
They need to reflect the right attitude.
They need not to offend the right people.
They need to be just other versions
of what is already being put out;
sloganized, religionized, traditionalized,
nationalized and indigenousized
thought currents
that must read like a nation
building itself
brick by brick.

And of course
it needs to be another labour of passion.
There will be no money.
Poets don't get paid here.
They don't even get read.

What's left is the across the sewage bridge
walk back to the room
to pray and chug in greatly
the chikozodo before sleeping
to wake up in vomit stained sheets
back to jobbing at the job.

LEFT HUNG OUT TO DRY
Mathews Mhango

In the midst of scorching heat, rivers of sweat flowed,
Struggling breath, our lungs suffocated and slowed.
As others gazed through windows, indifferent and dry,
Our bodies baked beneath the sun's merciless sky.

Their faces bore no pity, no remorse, no plight,
Sheltered in their comfort, cloaked in economic light.
The hot ground beneath burned our dry, cracked feet,
Our shackled dreams failed to soar to shadows of comfort

The thirst of our dry throat crying in complete silence,
As the rivers of sweat have salted our cracked faces.
Through pristine glass dome they see us from their perfect world,
As we hang dry on ropes of solitude, scars etched with pain.

Behind the windows, they smiled, feasting from fountain of plenty,
The savory taste of their feast, blinding them to our reality.
They feasted while we withered, as the winds froze our skin,
Our patience, like our bodies was broken from within.

SILENT SCARS
Mathews Mhango

The pain of these wounds burned like wildfire,
Scorching the fragile walls of my broken heart.
I wandered, lost in shadows,
Alone in a dark forest of persistent pain.
This torment, inflicted on me,
Plays like a continuous trailer of horror,
Haunting my nights—sleepless nights.
It scares me, afraid it might come back.
The silence of my solemn cries
Echoes through the chaos of your brutality.
I live among crumbling foundations,
Hoping for a hand,
To pull me from this hell.
But I am left alone,
While others point at the scars of my anguish.
The pain from these scars
Is unbearable.
Please, don't return
To make my soul melt in fear again.
Through the drawings of my scars,
I still hear echoes of your torture,
Conveying a message of your brutality deep within.
Yet I must survive this pain,
Praying these chains will break in no time.
Like a blooming flower in resistance,
I will Shine brighter than ever before.

And rise above this anguish, this stigma,
To disgrace the hands that carved these scars.

TWO SHOTS OF PAIN
Mathews Mhango

I walked into this bar....
Let me take these two shots of pain,
Sprinkled with lemon sorrow.
Maybe I'll drink away the insult.

I stirred in silence,
Hoping this cocktail
Could drown my guilt and shame.

I sipped on echoes of my own voice
As the jukebox played my guilty song.
The barstool next to me
Still warm with my ghost.

Others around me danced in joy
Sipping cocktails of laughter and light....
While mine was
A pint of anger to numb the ache.

I tried to join them on the floor,
But my body couldn't match the beat....
This joyful rhythm

Was foreign to limbs soaked in regret.

So, I resigned myself to the counter,
Hoping the barman would keep pouring….
Indulging this solemn version of me,
Letting the liquor blur the ghosts in my mind.

Each sip tore
Like a memory down my throat.
Even the mirror behind the bar
Didn't recognize me anymore

DRUM OF PEACE

Ophoke Leonard Onyebuchi

As lions clutch their faces
    The patient deer hung so gently
        Panting to have their daily bread
            Lines apart
                Thus unite
                  5

A blazing heart
    Hunted for joy
        Like a charming maiden
            Calling for attention
              4

Patients though
    Hard as rock
        All the same
            Longing for chill
            4

The joy of the moonlight
    Flashing lights of the stars
        Melos the chamber
            Of my beast
            4

A cracked hole
                              Moist mud
                                Stained
                        garment
                           Rage of tigers
                      Canopy of trees
                  Hosts of termites
              Multitude of ants
          Gangs of terror
      Dragons of disaster
   Echoing
Enough!
            11

The leopard's skin
Untouched by rain
Softens the rocks
Soothing the bones
Whispering fragrant
Words of peace.
            6

Waning Crown, Mother Land!

Ophoke Leonard Onyebuchi

Must I be your silent martyr?
Mother of shining lands,
Cradle of lions, life in your hands.
Africa's song and flame,
Savannah wide, rivers untamed
Yet you repay me with silent shame.   6

I robed you in green and golden grace,
Umbrella trees in warm embrace.
Baobabs rose to kiss the sky,
Elephants roamed, the eagles cried
A kingdom proud in every eye.   5

Now rage ignites my weary bones,
You strip my crown, you crush my thrones.
Flood and drought, a brutal pair,
My veins run dry, my lungs gasp air.
The cradle of life becomes despair.   5

Yet hush! A whisper through the trees,
A promise riding on the breeze.
Plant again, let rivers mend,
Where greed began, let mercy end.
And watch my wounded soul ascend.   5

Was I carved for such a sorrow?
A continent betrayed by trust.
But hearts renewed can heal these scars,
And lift my spirit past the stars.
To birth anew what once was ours. 5

Uniting Africa's Children

Ophoke Leonard Onyebuchi

In the shade of nations, diverse and vast,
A mother's love is a tie that will forever last.
My mother, not better than any other's embrace,
Speaks in tongues, a harmonious cultural grace.
    4

Swahili, Luganda, and Igbo's embrace,
Ateso whispers, languages interlace,
These threads of her power, diversity's kiss,
My mother is special, unique in her bliss.
    4

"Little child," she responded with care,
"A mother's love is meant to be shared.
For a mother is more than blood and bone,
A life giver, a fighter, seeds she's sown.
    4

She keeps us in view, come joy or strife,
Shielding her children, the center of life.
If I depart, and my children survive,
Their smiles shall brighten the world, come alive. 4

I am the mother of children, the continent wide,
In me, they find strength, in me, they confide.
When I bleed, it's for Africans' plight,
In laughter, I celebrate their might.
    4

When I rain, it's blessings I send,
In the kitchen, love's flavors blend.
I'm a mother, limitless, no boundaries in sight,
In my heart, you're my day and my night.
    4

My sons and daughters, heed my decree,
I'm a mother for all, as you can see.
Speak in tongues, embrace black and white,

Walk, fly, and never lose sight.

    4

Of the tears you shed, and the strength to repair,
For in unity and love, you're a power to bear.
A cloth for the naked, bread for the hungry,
A shared sorrow, a future that's sunny.

    4

Solidarity, together you stand,
Chasing division away from your land.
I am a mother to all, my children of birth,
Learn from my love, unite the Earth.

    4

In this competition, let Africa's voice ring clear,
A mother's love, her children hold dear.
For in her embrace, they find a home,
Not a war den, but a place to freely roam.

    4

POETICS OF THE POETS
Usman Danjuma Osu

To find purifying performance
to gain optical sights
to fossilize falsehood romance
to eschew black ties,
let washer men enclose detergent
For purpose of purgation.
He is judged intelligent
if he embraces regulation.
Restless desperation begets search
where wisdom is found.
Where molders embrace research.
Philosophic foundations are sound
Insightful check cheques not dubitable dimple
milking healthy community's breast nipple.

WHO LOVES THE MATCH?
Usman Danjuma Osu

Who loves to watch the match?
This accoladious though restive catch;
the performance of interlock romance
Bearing arms with never ready arms
Between that actively pacing pranking identity.
Armed to harm and to support hefty passivity
attracted by feeling adequately common
as the players heart woke to summon
the uncoordinated, though hefty adage
"Mourning each morning" with our eagle's message
to our nations governed by clown
An honourarium decked by frown
when shall we exhume heroism
to rake-off glutting fanaticism?

SHOULD WE FORGIVE VEGETABLE LOVE?
Usman Danjuma Osu

In vegetable growth speed indeed
we sprout like light speed rate seed
Our love sits on marks of bliss
giving each meter no space to cease
its weight of healthy companionship
after all, we are good meant for fellowship.
We are still less than spelling 'Robinson',
why forgetting to garnish the winsome
and turning our grim dream to dim?
Don't we know what to redeem?
We are wearing the wax's watts
we blow and bow our face to darts
rather than our leaping higher as an AMAZON
we cringe before the mire of dying axiom.

STAR, PERSONIFIED
Bucknor Esther

She stood there, a sole glim in the dark night. She had released her hair from its confines; they sang of freedom in the gentle breeze. A loose, diaphanous gown shimmered down to jade-white feet, long pristine scarf swaddled twinlike heaps.
How bright she was, even the stars sat in her eyes. Real, sparkling specks scattered over melancholic purple. She bore a sword, no happier than she wore a frown. In her hand, it hung down by her side, just as her smile hung down on both sides. She was brightness that wrought destruction. Like a comet caught in action.

FAR ENOUGH FOR TWO
Bucknor Esther

Inner strength.
He said if you dropped out early, then you
lacked inner strength.
Seeing her lay on her bed, I think she'd finally
lacked it.
Her brows fell. But not for debility, for
livid fury. Her lips rose to the full height of a
sneer, and she said to me,
"Do I lack it really? With such a friable heart
as this. Do you know the extent of the blows
dealt it? Only a star glimpsed when I nearly
broke down in a street where souls flittered
past.
Nobody glimpsed when I flung myself
into a dark, tiny space, clutching my slacks
like I clutched self-control. When my chest
erupted with shudders and fervid lava
seared my vision, leaving trembling flesh
in its wake.
When I wrestled my ego and kept its head
bowed, declaring training the winner and king.
When my boldness' fingers quivered
as I proffered a bright smile.
When, eyes trailing after disappointment
as it flounced past, I silenced emotion.
When I bit the tongue that aided my thoughts

trickle down my throat, forgotten.
Still, I stand fast here, polishing armour
and refurbishing arsenal.
So be gone with all of that.
For I've got inner strength, and far enough
for two."

FRAGMENTS THAT SELFLESSLY FORGE YOU
Bucknor Esther

You have a painter's eye
and a dancer's quake,
a singer's gleam
and a sculptor's ache.
A sketcher's dream
and a jeweler's spark,
a florist's colour
and an orchestra's allure.
A maestro's charm
and a cellist's fingers,
a writer's caution
and a poet's abandon.
Hence, I call you,
Art.

SOMETIME IN JUNE
Denis Waswa Barasa

Smoke splits through the silent streets
Like lightning
The piercing cracking sounds
Mixed with minced muffled
Cries of protesters
Cling to the edges of the city
Like mud on the boots of soldiers
Plodding through Moorish terrain
In silence
Birds flee
In silence
The silent street screams
In silence
The clock counts
In silence
The screaming street
Splashed and splattered
And splintered with blood
Bears
The sirens
Bears
The crimson blood
The walls witness with wails
The desolate pleas of the protesters
They drop
Dead.

The boots bully the streets
Guns, grenades, gangrene
Grill the once peaceful populace
Ambulance sirens
Military sirens
Police sirens
Sirens. Silence. Screams.

The evening news are eerie with ire
Loud silence of missing subjects
Mammoth mounts of mottled
Mutilated men
Screens are scarred with scary scenes
Fury furrowed in flaming fumes
Anger ambled in anguish
A generation guillotined, gutted
Dreams dashed
For daring to imagine
A better nation
They are stilled
Killed.

Silence swirls from the State
For the suffering seeking answers
Chilling silence
For the missing minors
The maimed
Cold mumbling murmurs.

Young shoots are abloom
Through the crevices they push
Lilies line the streets
Roses resist the rust
Daisies daintily declare
A season of Hope
Sometime in June
There was withering
Sometime in June
Freedom will blossom.

The Rain Came
Denis Waswa Barasa

Like a sparrow in the sky
So confident and cool
Is my desire for rain.

The wind blew
The blue sky grew dark
The trees swayed
And the goats bleated
Doors banged and windows whacked
We children cheered
As the birds chirped
Fleeing to their nests

In drizzles the rain drew
Soon it was a raspy rhythm
The baby slept
And the tank grew full
Down in torrents the rain poured
It was soon wet
What once was dry and warm.

Slowly, the drops dulled
Outside was a pool
Ducks and swans were enthralled
Life for them had become cool.

The rain had come and gone
Leaving us cold to the bone
And the earth soaked to the stone.

The sky was turning grey
And soon will be back to blue
And the breeze will still blow
The chill away
We will be warm again
After the rain.

The Bat
Denis Waswa Barasa

He flaps his wings
Behind the leaves
Out goes the light
And in he flies in the wings.

I follow him
To whence he hides in the day
Upside down I see him hang
Half asleep and half awake
He's half a bird and half a cat!
What magic be this
I wonder!

I throw a stone at the site
And he's swift on his flight
Is he a bird
This bat
Or is he a cat
I wonder!

When darkness drives the day away
Birds to their nests make their way
But busy bats soon on the way
Like the milky way paint the sky
Are they birds
These bats

Or are they cats
I wonder!

Existence in the Vacuum
Susan Gamuchirai Muchirahondo

We have wrote stories
We have bode farewall
We have sought comfort
We have sought peace and safety

The human race
A remarkable species that has managed to travel across the oceans
and fly in the air
And yet
Procreation persists
Nuptials are signed and ommitted to
Companionship
A hot commodity that has inspired so much invetion and
creativity

I love you
The first telephone
The first light bulb
The apple that fell from a tree and brought gravity to light

All key events that turn a world upside down and the beginning of a new era

I have set sail
Amidst storms
Travelled through a world of pain and seen the beauty of the moments that took my breath away
The moments that shed light

Is it crazy
That the toughest journey we travel is one to be loved?
By masses or individuals
By a deity

And that in a world full of so many people
So many similar beings
When we travel it's solo travlleing regardless of how many people are on the same boat as you?
But isn't it amazing
That though it may be a solo trip
You can scream out and grab someone when the ship's about to sink?

Affinity
Susan Gamuchirai Muchirahondo

You are reality
A force of gravity
When I was up in arms
Up in air
In dark space
You are lifeline to ship afloat and sinking
You are sturdy ground
You are muse to poet
You are star dust in dark nights
You are flavour to new ground
You are spice and everything nice
You are hero to damsel at the edge of edges
You are ecstasy in warm nights
You are woodwarmth in winter
You are solid
You are chip off the old block of consistency
You are the feel of company
Warm hugs and mild kisses
Soft words and gentle manner
You are everything but not most things
You are mine.

War cry
Tanatswa Nyamayaro

Eerie sounds of wailing
Echoed through the abyss
And there, huddled together
Surrounding a crackling fire
Whose leaping tongues brought back nostalgic memories
Of days when the invader
Called me a stranger in my own home
And sucked my land high and dry
When I think of those times....
Until one day a war cry reverberated
From Tanganyika to Dzimbabwe
Talk of the insurgence
Amayo! Those were the times

With mucus greased cheeks
And hope in our souls
We bade farewell to thee
These cracked hands still remember
The feel of the bazooka
As it roared in anger
And spit fire
In unison with the beholder
A sweet lyric in our hearts
África, mother, freedom is rebirth

Almost Christmas
Tanatswa Nyamayaro

Aloof on the mountain top
Engulfed by the humid air
Dense with the promise of rain
Was a crackling fire, under a huge oak tree
There sat the patriarch
Perched on an oak stool
A brood of grandchildren hovering around him
A scintillating aroma filled flaring nostrils
Emerging from smoke filled huts
Where distant aunts and in-laws made a culinary show
Amid playful banter

Four suspecting goats watched with interest
Their fate unbeknownst to them
As I yielded a large blade
Looking for who to devour
Children with rosy cheeks sped past
Pupils dilated in excitement
Indeed, it was almost Christmas

The Mirror Lied
Ifechieme Chima-Ogoke

The mirror told me I was cracked,
That beauty left and never came back.
It showed a girl with tired eyes,
Wearing shame like a thin disguise.

It whispered lines I never said,
Painted scars that I had shed.
Each glance became a silent scream
A broken face in a shattered dream.

But mirrors don't know how hearts are made,
They fade with fog, their truths decay.
They see the surface, miss the flame,
And wrap our souls in someone else's name.

I am more than what is shown
A storm of strength I call my own.
My skin may bend, my hair may fall,
But I still rise through it all.

So now I speak, I lift my head,
No more lies where light has spread.
The mirror lied, but I forgive
I choose to heal. I choose to live.

The Child I Used to Be
Ifechieme Chima-Ogoke

I miss her
The barefoot girl who danced in the rain,
Who laughed without reason,
Who believed the moon followed her home.

I see her now in windows,
In puddles, in old birthday cards,
But she stares at me like a stranger
As if I left her behind.

She used to dream with both eyes open, Count stars, not scars.
She wasn't afraid of mirrors
Or silence
Or goodbye.

I traded her giggle for grown-up words, Swapped crayons for questions,
Lullabies for long nights
And hope…
For hard truths.

But still

Sometimes I find her In a whisper,
In the soft hug of a memory.
She hasn't gone.
She just waits…
For me to believe again.

The Voice I Found
Ifechieme Chima-Ogoke

They told me silence was safety,
That speaking would shatter things.
So I swallowed my truth
And wore my wounds like jewellery.

But inside me,
A voice began to grow
 Not loud at first,
Just a whisper in the ribs.

It hummed through pain, Through every no,
Through every moment I forgot
That I was enough.

It sang when I almost gave up,
It rose when I wanted to shrink. And one day,
I didn't whisper back.
I roared.

I found the voice I buried
The one shaped like fire and forgiveness,
Like poetry and protest,
Like freedom and faith.

Now I speak.
Not because I have no fear

But because I found the voice That fear could not kill.

The warrior of Likoma
Immulanie Makande

The most dreaded warrior of our village
cannot sit by himself.
He's suffering from persistent diarrhea
of the mind.
His once protuberant belly
now muffled,
as if he holds no insides.
He can't feed himself, his hands
fragile like the skin of yolk.
The body that frightened us all
dances to children songs,
polished by, not bull's urine;
but yoghurt and porridge.
Our Morena
kneels for chameleons,
catches grasshoppers for lizards,
trades warrior songs
for maize and beans.
Tell him to stop this nonsense
He will grow back his crawls.
Bring him mud from the river
He will roar his head off.
Boil him a single clove
He will uproot the tree.

Bury me where
David Chasumba

When I breathe my last
And return to dust
Bury me where
I kiss the ground
Like Dambudzo Marechera
Returning from exile,
Bury me where
No one asks me,
'Where are you from?'
Where no one spews hate
On crowded trains
Where proximity isn't a threat
And we chat freely on buses
And no one calls me a mugger
Bury me where neighbours greet me
With a handshake and warm hug
And chat about good old days
Bury me where people don't stare
Like I'm an alien from another planet
Where people don't have talking eyes
That remind me I'm other
From a dark and different mother,
Bury me where neighbours don't leave
Sticky notes on my wind screen
Warning me of parking in wrong space,
Bury me where no one calls the cops

Coz the volume on my stereo is loud,
Bury me where I walk proud
With a swagger and a draught lager
Where my umbilical cord was cut
And buried in the ground
Where my ancestors rest
Where mother showered me with love
And I found teenage love

When I breathe my last
And return to dust
Bury me where
My spirit can revisit
The dusty streets I played
The mango tree I climbed
The childhood house I lived
And bed I laid
Bury me where
I can dream of the cold lands
I rested and nested,
Then like an old migrant bird
I flew back home to converge
And land in the sand

You make me laugh
David Chasumba

(For Anesu)

You make me laugh
When my day has been rough
When you nudge me, and whisper,
'Grand dad, wake up.'
And you mimic my snoring
Like a hippo grunting
You make me laugh
When you make those funny faces
And play tickle tickle with me
When you try plucking
Grey hairs off my head.
I still laugh today
When I recall that sunny day
In Stratford-upon-Avon
When we posed under the huge statue
For a selfie, and you said,
'Grand dad, tell that man up there to come down.'
I laughed till my ribs hurt
Then finally replied,
'Sorry, sweetheart, that man can't come down.
That's Willian Shakespeare, the famous English playwright.'
You make me laugh
When you scurry up the stairway
Knowing that's naughty

But you push the boundaries anyway
Because you know you can
When at Grandad and Gogo's home,
You make me laugh
When we go to the park
And you make us chase after you
And you tell your dad
To go back to mum
So that you could be free
To take risks on rides,
You make me laugh
When you are reading to us
And teaching us
How to pronounce the word 'Tomato'.
You make me laugh
When you go into character
Playing the role of Dr. Anesu
Measuring my temperature
And giving me flu shots.

You make me laugh
When my day has been sad
Above all, you make me ponder
About childhood innocence
And make me see
The world closer or yonder
Through curious three-year-old eyes.

Sowing in Tears
David Chasumba

Blessed is the hungry farmer
Tilling the drought-stricken land
And sowing in tears,
Blessed is the barren woman
Supplicating at sunset
And sowing in tears,
Blessed is the poor orphan
Burning the midnight candle
And sowing in tears,
Blessed is the ex-convict
Mending his crooked ways
And sowing in tears,
Blessed is the freedom fighter
Fighting the beautiful struggle
And sowing in tears,
Blessed is the activist
Choking on tear gas
Yet standing up for justice
And sowing in tears,
Blessed is the street vendor
Selling sweets by the road side
In scorching September sun
And sowing in tears

Blessed is everyone sowing in tears
In the dry seasons of hardship, distress

Famine and personal trials,
For the season of harvest will come
To dry the rivers of tears
And the farmer will reap the soy
And Hannah will kiss baby Samuel
And the orphan will publish his verse
And the ex-convict will teach wayward sons
And the freedom fighter will rule the land
And the activist will preach **Black Lives Matter**
And the street vendor will shed tears of joy
When her boy walks the podium.

N.B- This poem was inspired by Psalm 126:5, 'Those who sow with tears will reap with songs of joy.'

BABYLON
Sithembele Xhegwana

From third word to first world,
from periphery to centre
 From rural to urban,
from township to suburb,
From dust to concrete,
from oil lamps to street lamps,
From pine to pine,
from sky to sky,
I have come.

From the broken village,
I have come to this place of robots,
crowded by fruit and flower sellers,
This city choked with taxis,
their drivers hooting,
screaming.

The beggars on the kerbs pushing
their trolleys, mobile homes,
The street children in the doorways,
 stoned for the winter night.
From the city now I go back
to the townships where robbers
demand their life's share,

where drug lords knock

from door to door, where
police officers are also directors
of crime, and women open their
thighs for survival. On the way
I pass monuments Victorian, Georgian,
colonial, I pass tourists, grinning, sleek.
There are the suburbs where the wealthy
 recline,

Where their children ride horses,
swim. From third world to first world,
from periphery to centre,
From rural to urban,
from township to suburb,
from dust to concrete,
from oil lamps to street
lamps, from pine to pine,

from sky to sky, I have come
Here where I cannot change
what has been, where I sing
anthems from a no longer heroic
age, that of the slaughtered King
Sarhili's and King Hintsa's.
Here, where my past dwindles
and the village dies.

VOICES IN THE WIND
Sithembele Xhegwana

Voices in the wind
Accompany me in my adventures.
They tell me a million stories;
They speak to me gently. As
I press my feet against the
cracks of these gravel roads,
These voices riddle the sand
and the dust. As I retrace my
steps in the dark blue enigma
of the Muncushe streams,
They give me stories: cadences.

"No, I don't believe in you," I
retort; I try to duck their giant
steps. The voices persist, tell
 me a million stories: stories
of the original fall in Eden,
stories of man's grandeur
in Babel, stories of King
Hintsa's skull and Nongqawuse's
legend. I raise my hand, persisting,
"I do not want to listen."

These voices shrug off my many
protests. The stories unfold, the
narrative swells: more cadences.

When one mentions King Shaka
Zulu, I lift up the dusty coils of
my ears; when I hear of Nxele and
Maqoma, working in the Cape
docks, and of Siyolo and Xhexho,
Coming to the Cape in chains
to build the Break Water Prison,
And of Nelson and Robert,
crumbling in the island, I weep,
I weep.

"I must have lost my mind
To be even communicating
with such," These voices gush
out anyway, they drown me:
voices in the wind. They order
me to retell these stories. I say,
"Take it easy pal, I still have my
democratic rights." These voices
just smile and fade from conscious-
ness. They transcend the great
abyss between stone and sky,
from where, I suppose,
they came. And I am left
alone, shrilling and sinking.

The prize
Justice Masangano

In the howling, ever gathering clouds
And the ensuing storm
Rolling over the mountains
I crawl
Past wooden walls, doors closing
A forgotten child

My mother,
Closing the shattered window
Sees me from a distance
Tired, weak, trying,
Hope lost.

In her big shawl,
She steps into the cold
Her face wrinkled with pain
And whisks me up, tight
Striking my hair softly.

River rock
Justice Masangano

Centuries unaccounted now, still it nestle
A serene pause, quite confident along
The river bank like a sleeping giant watching
The water gurgling downstream, it's
Complexion brown, silver, bronze. It's skin,
Ragged and weather-beaten. It's body shape,
Curvy.
Between her invincible lips lies a platonic smile,
Beckoning, genuine, down to Earth.
Seasons upon seasons, dawns upon dawns
Couples have come, crossing hills, walking
Valleys, jumping gullies to paint on it love emojis
Which have survived a hell of torrential rain
And hold each other in their arms while listening
To bird-songs, the chirp of cicadas, the bleat of
Livestock and the croak of frogs, the

blend of their
Rhythm matchless
And they still come, bold and confident
To touch, to smile and laugh together
But I am that fisherman who travel miles and miles
And sit on it always with a fishing line in my hand

The belly of the beast
Justice Masangano

To the hostility of unwelcome struggle,
Death-tolls and trouble
I never packed up my belongings
But left in a helluva hurry
The place where my ancestors lived for generations
Not sure whether to return
When the tsunami calms down.
I wonder
If all those souls;
Often weak and exhausted
The rich, the poor, villagers, city dwellers, old men, women, infants...
Who joined us along the way;
On foot, on jam-packed oxen and lorries...
In the scorching sun sweating
And in the cold winter shivering
Arrived at their destinations
Perhaps I am one of those lucky one's
A testimony of a stark exodus.

Looking Straight Into My Eyes
Moore Ngwenya

Always telling me with pride filled
with jealousy.
With your eyes burning fury at my
Smiling cheeks.
Mocking your unending ways of
disdainfulness .
Concealed by the sugar coated words
of appraisal.
Spitted whilst looking straight into
My eyes .

Slipping from on looking eyes wishing
to ambush.
The far seen ambitions of the past.
Yet building a barrier of unseen ignorance
sealed in their hearts.
As they run around confirming every trail
of my tracks.
As they gather into clusters of gossip .
Giving out futile reports of success trickled
by improvement.
As their waves spread till the news reach the
back of my ears.
Looking Straight Into My Eyes

Standing in every corner of the road I lay a

Foot on.
With a steely gaze they frown at my every
Approaching steps.
As they greet me with great enthusiasm
Mocking my perseverance.
Concealed by the sugar coated words of
Appraisal .
Spitted whilst looking straight into my eyes.

Rumblings
Raphael Onyejizu

(for Gabriel Okara)
(I)
Drums do not rumble across the tropical savannah at ease,
Nor do they recede in the silent nights of the vast mangrove.
From the macabre of maddening months, the mammoth misses
Its limbs to the creaky caveats creeping into the colossal caves.
The wind set sails across the Niger lush lands of Giant udders,
The Northern enclaves of vast agrarian lands twirl to twitching tilts.
Its Carnery bird lays the fiery ball-dung of conflicting and warring eggs,
With bayonets of militia Haramists and herdsmen, vaunting the verdicts
Of violence for volcanos, erupted in the epoch of boko-fanatics.
(II)
The cyclone twirls across the Middle Belt district of the Benue valleys,
Where puff adders spit lethal venoms of ethnic rift for natives and nomads,
The discord that trades ill-winds for terrors, tremours and moulting magmas.
For the inhabitants of Jos to Makurdi, the Birom-Idoma-Tiv heartlands,
A gory tale wells from the relics of death's fragments, a wily usurper of joy!
A hundred kill for a hundred grave begets no ditties for peacemakers,

As watchers who bewail the maladies of murderous machetes, mime to mourn.
He who kills for wrathful devotion awaits the dangers of reprisal contentions.
(III)
The typhoon stretches its arms from the wild west-scapes to the Lagoons,
Scalping earth cracks for serrated seeds beneath the ruinous landscape.
Amotekun's thunderbird rose above the tidal feasts of war mongers,
Whose plucky duel is to the furtive lore, a tripod web that makes to mars?
The Fulanizers of ours will do grope grimly with the guts of gauntlets,
To deprecate the couple's oatmeal of our unity turned into a brawl,
That guzzles the termite-like festals on the duodenal gullets of Wazobia.
Every arbiter knows when drumbeats recline for a cantos rave.
(IV)
The east heartlands of the rising sun unveil its stormy tongues of rage,
There, the python danced its thighs out in ceaseless gyms and gyres.
For liberty's quest sprang molehills to rebel on the iron chest of oppression,
From the viral idioms of a self-acclaimed Superman, Nnamdi Kanu.

Let not the musketeers of cruelty fret, for fortune did favour freedom fighters,
When on time's inquest, a century's herald gathers the moss of consents,
To part ways as comrades from the hinterland of pro-secessionist agitations.
He who divides a morsel for all must learn to stake with equity and justice.

(V)

The monsoon surges across the Delta regions of dense forest grooves,
Where egrets of black gold fed no mean natives and multinationals.
From the outcries of oil spill, black soots and aged war towards its dwellers,
The Ijaw-Ogoni axis drew blood in sea-bound bunkers, gunboats and armoury.
Since coercion fosters the fastidious furrow that compels obedience,
For wrongs unjustly enabled by power brokers at the conclave of the cabals.
Where drums fail to relapse at this blighted bloc of strife and folly,
Chaos may birth newborns for those who stride into a dreamland of Hitlers.

Sahara Run
Raphael Onyejizu

(for victims of illegal migration)

In this hot chase & r a c y v o y a g e along acrid Sahara desert,
Parched c a r c a s s e s of skulls & rotten fleshes are spotted.
F r a g m e n t s of migrant bodies defaced by heaving heat &
Bot flies, lay h e l p l e s s l y in the malodorous-scented winds of the wild.
There, the carrion v u l t u r e s feast firmly amidst the fuming sunrays,
& all that remains of the d e c a y i n g bodies of Africans who trudged
From Lybia to Europe, are s c o r c h e d black-brownish-looking fabrics,
Of dreary wild-eyed sockets, b r u i s e d-lips, maggot-ridden-mucus tongues,
Swollen-bellies-crinkled-limbs, b r o k e n-ribs-arid-bones, twisted nails,
Grey phalanges, split-feet-s a n d y hairs & a set of cackling yellow teeth,
Peeping through the d u s t y-c r u s t y-reddish-earth, such desolate relics,
Stack as hags of g h o s t l y silhouettes from the reliquaries of witches.
As the stormy h e a t Intensifies its fortes on torrid silts of eerie Komodos,
Loud cracks of r e e k i n g-creaking sound buckle to pact, the gory piece
Of a S a h a r a run, fated to a halt in a desert where brave souls freeze

Once, but l i v e d on as limping dancers to the cadences of fittest survivors.
They prod t h r o u g h the Northern route to the West, where fortune
Favours no black g u t s a m i d s t the crunch & cranky living from
Oddities of hard labours f o r m e a g r e Euros & hamburgers,
To muddling of self & d i s p a r i t i e s that await all migrants.

Wonders!

Raphael Onyejizu

No one wonders why this land licks its own blood
                With the smell of fresh bones filling the air.
                        First, it wakes us up to the
blasts of bombs.   Next, it
weighs us down with the roar of guns.
            Then, it harms us with the scene of m u t i l a t i o n
s…   Still, it hounds us with the flesh of
decapitations,   *Splattered on red
earth for termites to feed on.*

At *Adani, Afia, Bokkos, Owan, Omala*[1]…
            We are hunted down like bush fowls
With glazed machetés meant for cattle.
    We die each day like dogs with no owners,
        Decoding the stillness of silence;
            Silence that breeds the norm of
defiance.

This night wakes us up to sad news
        When the spirits dream out of their restful bodies
                At the sudden cough of the
Ak-rifles.   `   Just this
night, a mother searches for her children

---

[1] Rural communities in Enugu, Benue, Plateau, Edo, and Kogi States of Nigeria, pillaged by herdsmen crisis.

Only to find a heap of b e h e a d e d skulls,
        Soaked in a pool of their own blood.

Just this night, a father loses both legs
        To the flying axe of a skilful normad!
              He must learn to flee, or die crawling.   Just this night,
a village meets its ghost of memory;
        No safety, no security, no refuge to find shelter;
              No hope, no helper, no vigilant eyes to dowse its fears.

The next day shocks us
        With headlines we are unaccustomed to:
              TWENTY ABDUCTED! THIRTY KILLED!   FORTY MURDERED! SIXTY BUTCHERED!
NINTY MASSACRED! HUNDREDS DISPLACED!
        'In just two days?' *we ask, enraged...*
              What answers do we get? N o n e!

THE HEART IS A WILD ANIMAL
Paul Oluwafemi David

(1)
The heart is a wild animal
chained in the cages of our ribs.

It roars with voices called pulses
fighting for escape through death
every Second,
every Minute,
every Hour,and
every day.

The heart is a wild animal
bound in the Mediastinum of our chest .

It barks with voices called beats
raging for escape through death
every week,
every month and
every year.

It hunts the body, soul and the spirit
every second, minute, hour and day
as the apex predator with all
 its smooth muscles and blood supply
 relaxing through
atrial diastole mixed with isovolumic relaxation
and contracting through atrial mixed with

ventricular systole trying to devour our
life but light came to assist by shining
through its darkness.

It roars with voices screaming
as radial pulses on our wrist.
It barks with voices echoing
as carotid pulses on our neck.

For us to be aware of the battle
between light and darkness set
in motion with the blood
sacrifice of our birth.

(11)

1.2 roars in a second,
The heart is a wild animal.

72 roars in a minute,
The heart is a wild animal.

4320 roars in one hour,
The heart is a wild animal.

103680 roars in a day,
The heart is a wild animal.

It hunts the body, soul and spirit

every week, month and year
as the climax predator with all
its smooth muscles and blood supply
relaxing through atrial diastole mixed with
Isovolumic relaxation
 and contracting through atrial mixed with
ventricular systole trying to devour
our life but light came to assist by
shining through its darkness.

It roars with voices ringing
as femoral pulses on our groin.
It roars with voices knocking
as popliteal pulses on our knee.

For us to be conscious of the battle
between light and darkness set
in motion with the painful
tears of our delivery.

725,760 roars in a week,
The heart is a wild animal.

3110400 roars in a month,
The heart is a wild animal.

37843200 roars in a year,
The heart is a wild animal.
(111)

UMBILICAL CORD

(two arteries and a vein)
A pinch of honey was placed on your lips by
the priest during your naming ceremony to welcome
you into seven kingdoms.

In the morning you cried,
Father,I have never seen
the Sun since my solitude.

In the night you cried,
Mother,I have never seen
the Moon since my solitude.

Honey is immortal,
May your life be full of impact and intensity
after the fall of your umbilical cord.

Water has no enemy,
May your life be full of love and joy
after the fall of your umbilical cord.

Kolanut is chewed and spitted out,
May your life repel evil and darkness
after the fall of your umbilical cord.

Sugar is sweet,

May your life be full of freedom and liberty
after the fall of your umbilical cord.

Pepper has many seeds,
May your life be full of kings and queens
after the fall of your umbilical cord.

Palm oil is a lubricant,
May your life full of victory and glory
after the fall of your umbilical cord.

Salt is a seasoning,
May your life be full of taste and flavour
after the fall of your umbilical cord.

We love South Africa
Deena Padayachee

We are the simple citizens and residents of South Africa.
We don't need pomp and ceremony to make ourselves feel important.
For that we just need the quality of our work.

We are the simple taxpayers of South Africa.
We don't need luxurious limousines and pageantry to feel confident,
We do need love and the respect of our people.

We are the simple workers of South Africa,
We don't need suits and ties to feel dressed and valued,
We just need to feel good within ourselves.

We are the ordinary people of an extraordinary country.
We don't need mansions and servants to feel nice about our ourselves.
We just need happy and loving families who have respect in their eyes and love in their hearts.

We are the worried people of South Africa.
We don't need extravagant banquets, waste and condescending, ostentatious, exclusionary 'dignitaries'.
We cook the food, we clean the halls, we service the cars, we fix everything.

We don't need external glitter to conceal the deceit and the dishonour within some.

We are the peaceful people of South Africa,
We don't need free air travel and gifts to build our country,
But we do need first-class teachers and a first-class education system

and first-class police and an efficient legal system.

We are the proud patriots of South Africa.

We are in love with our people, our country, our Home.
We help our country all that we can.
We don't need statues, street names or photographs in government offices to feel important.
We do need respect, integrity, parsimony, and patriotism from the servants of the people.

We are simple South Africans.
We do need leaders who will listen more and do more,
Not dishonourable leaders who talk down to us, and look down on us,

and think that they are 'better' than us.

For this we hope, for this we pray,
Into this nirvana may our country rise like the blossoming of an African Protea,

Caring, kind and loving more than we can hope for.

Les Poèmes
Passez-moi des mots
Adamou Idé

Passez-moi des mots
Chaque main le sien
Pour écrire un poème

Passez-moi des mots
Non pas des mots lisses ou des mots policés
Non pas des mots qui sortent des eaux claires des piscines
Non pas des mots parfumés d'ambre, d'eau de rose
Ou d'autres suaves fragrances qui caressent les narines
Passez-moi des mots !

Passez-moi des mots
Des mots-flèches j'entends
Des mots qui ont grandi sur les tas d'immondices
Qui nous servent de greniers dans nos villes mystères
    Passez-moi des mots
Des mots-tambours
Couvés dans les cases mouroirs où ils sont nés
Des mots-flamme bleue
Des mots qui sortent des forges du peuple en colère
Passez-moi des mots
Pour interroger les seigneurs sur leurs promesses de bonheur

Passez-moi pour écrire un poème : des mots !
Non pas des mots lisses

Non pas des mots d'Athènes, de Rome ou de Paris
Pour faire érudit
Non pas des mots-parures qui brillent sur nos têtes
Non pas des mots endimanchés
Ou des mots sages et peureux
Mais des mots-cris que j'entends
Au détour de nos rues sombres
Où s'écrit la mort avec une lame perfide
Des mots-cris que j'entends dans le vacarme des bombes
Des mots qui montrent les flancs maigres des femmes
Errant sur les chemins d'exil
    Des mots !
Des mots que je sens, enfants des soufflets du maître fou
Sur nos joues creuses
Dans les salles obscures des tortures
Passez-moi des mots !

Passez-moi des mots
Forces qui décuplent ma force
Forces qui protègent les enfants qui dorment
Sevrés de leurs rêves
Passez-moi des mots
Chaque main le sien !

Passez-moi, pour écrire un poème : des mots !
Des mots-colombes pour laver mon cœur
De toute haine ou colère
Des mots pour la fête
Des mots pour un poème aquarelle

Pour me libérer de moi-même
Pour apporter la bonne nouvelle
Des jours heureux qui s'en viennent

Passez-moi des mots
Des mots qui adoucissent les vents
Des mots !
Pour hisser les grands voiles
Sur le vaste océan de la liberté

Passez-moi des mots
Par vos mains fraternelles
Chaque main le sien !

Les Dictateurs
Adamou Idé

Il court le feu dans nos poitrines
Brûlant les paroles sublimes qui nous avaient séduits
Brûlant le peu de rêves qu'ils nous avaient promis
Les Néron d'Afrique se rient de nos colères
Encerclant nos rues avec des sbires en treillis
Ils toisent le peuple avec mépris

Ils ont caché sous les cendres
Les mortelles envies qu'ils couvaient en secret
Ils ont oublié sur le feu du feu qu'ils appellent de tous leurs vœux
Les marmites pleines de haine qui s'énervent à présent…
Déjà des poings levés parées de machettes !
Déjà la danse funèbre des hommes au son des mitraillettes !
Déjà sur les chemins d'exil les femmes en deuil comptent les disparus !

Ils ont oublié les contes et les paraboles de nos grands-mères
Les tendres sourires de nos mères, les caresses sur nos têtes
Nos visages de gamins épanouis autour d'un feu doux
Ils ont oublié l'hymne à la paix que nous chantions au petit matin
Ils ont oublié que sous les larmes du peuple digne et fier
Coulent les sources profondes d'un bonheur qui échappe à leurs yeux

Ils ont oublié d'oublier nos querelles
La douceur des mots simples qui rafraîchissent nos cœurs

Ils ont oublié que dans nos tombes qu'ils creusent
De leurs griffes de rapaces
Les abeilles font le miel
Et travaillent à leur perte : les rois sanguinaires d'Afrique !

Poète, reviens !
Adamou Idé

Trop de bruit
Trop de cliquetis
Trop de bruit, de youyous inutiles
Trop de rires triomphants sur le suaire des serments
Voici les hommes en transes qui dansent sur le rythme du baril
Et les mains sûres de la nuit battent la mesure
Argent, money, blé, espèces, chèque, flouze no time to loose
Danse funèbre
Funeste frénésie sur les rives du Dow Jones
Où s'échouent nos paroles fraternelles
Trop de bruit
Même les maisons closes ne vendent plus l'amour
Mais des gémissements nocturnes de douleur contenue

Poète, infatigable ciseleur de jours, reviens !
Rien n'est définitivement écrit sauf ta liberté
Recueille patiemment les cendres dispersées de l'espoir
Dans le trou noir de nos mémoires
C'est là qu'ont lieu, sur des poteaux de fortune
Les exécutions sommaires de nos rêves légitimes
Poète, résiste !
Retrempe ta plume dans la jeunesse éternelle de nos regards
L'aube victorieuse des mots dans les ciels aquarelles
Prend forme à nouveau sous tes doigts d'accoucheur
Sur l'isthme de la beauté : lève-toi, poète !
Appelle les hommes

Et chante de ta voix claire l'antithèse de la haine
Poète : reviens !

L'idéal
Dan Mbo Kuba

Selon les étapes,
Avec un but précis,
L'on est sans cesse porté,
Par un idéal particulier;
Cette petite flamme,
Qui ne reste éteint,
Et qui sans cesse,
Nous porte vers l'avenir ;
Rien qu'avec la parole,
Que l'expression évoque,
Une prise simple ou même engageante,
La détermination;
Selon les modes et les moeurs,
Qu'un mouvement guidant,
Vers ce que l'on conçoit mieux,
Et qui reste pour toujours ;
Faire ce que l'on sait,
Reste une valeur morale,
Pour se faire respecter,
Malgré le collectif ;
L'apprentissage est idéal,
Demeure un positionnement,
Tant pour son bien,
Mais aussi de sa communauté.

Qui s'éveille
Dan Mbo Kuba

A la fois douce et ardente,
Lumineuse et indocile,
Qui passe par le fait,
D'un recensement epelant ;

Les mots viennent en lave,
Pour arriver à la hauteur,
Même dos au mur,
Un pastis de travers et mal dit;

L'on se tapes,
Comme si de rien n'était,
Quand le magma s'enfuit,
De la résonance de la chaleur;

L'inconfort se ressent,
Sur le cœur et les tripes,
Augmentant le taux vibratoire,
Une agressivité qui change de mode ;

Il faudra bien les dogmes,
Sans effacer et laisser un monde de joie,
Fruits de notre humanité,
Tel un espace de liberté et d'expression ;

Le chagrin et la sincérité,

Se bercent avec fidélité,
De cœur tendre et magnifique,
Qui rend fort et valeureux.

Le chemin du partage
Dan Mbo Kuba

Reflexion directe,
Pour tirer des leçons et grandir,
Guide de compassion,
Crucial et honnête ;

Ensemble pour chercher des solutions,
Sans susciter des frustrations ou des regrets,
Tant accablante ou incertaine,
Laissant l'espace à la bienveillance ;

Tant dans la vérité et sans jugement,
Authentique et simple,
Refuge doux et rassurant,
Perfection factice ou dans le fait ;

De ces instants de vulnérabilité,
Les plus imparfaites pour accueillir,
dégage une différence immense,
Pour écouter avec un coeur ouvert ;

Le plus beau cadeau à offrir,
Est ce lien inestimable,
Fait de l'amitié,
Un véritable havre de paix ;

Sans être une possession,

Des points s'acceptent,
Telles qu'elles sont,
Une identité similaire ;
Le tout sans hésiter,
Moment de s'abandonner,
Sans être coincée contre le mur,
Dont seul remède est l'amour ;

Sans reflet de fracture,
Postures logiques,
Qui frappent de part et d'autre,
Quête de stabilité de l'autre ;

Construction de solidarité,
De l'intégration,
Qui trace le chemin,
D'un choix allié ;

Sans laisser place au doute,
Ni se faire sentir sous-évalué,
Se rappeller de vos mérites,
Devoir d'action pleine ;

Garder précieusement,
Une mémoire sans escale,
Autour d'une discussion,
En son fort intérieur ;

Engagement et dévouement,

Pour tendre aux pratiques de partage,
A chemin droit,
Sans perdre son repère ;
Pour éclairer le chemin commun,
Adhérer au sens du service,
Sans cesse théorie abstraite,
Mais usage de bonne conscience.

La maîtresse de Dieu
Fraubi Amel

La maîtresse de Dieu
Était tout sauf une Sainte
Tellement belle des orteils aux cheveux
Que la terre la convoitait et s'en foutait du Maître

Je l'ai vu plusieurs fois cette maîtresse
Officier la messe aux quatre coins des rues
En rendant les hommes pécheurs, les femmes pécheresses
Tant, elle se marrait même de son homme, ce Témoin méconnu

Pourtant bien connu des inconnus de l'ombre du mal
Bénévole engagée de la moelle épinière jusque dans l'âme
La maîtresse de Dieu était bien exceptionnelle
Elle était née depuis l'époque d'Ève et d'Adam

Tout le monde n'est pas censé me comprendre
C'est ainsi et je n'en voudrais jamais à personne
Juste que je me dois de vous le faire apprendre
Afin que ma tête ne me punisse ou ne me raisonne

Sa maîtresse, tenez-vous bien enfin
C'est cette haine que tu nourris au fond de toi
C'est cette méchanceté humaine que je décris en vain
C'est bien sûr cette chaîne qui te lie aux sans foi ni loi

C'est ce pauvre qui te sourit et que tu mines
C'est cet enfant que tu frappes avec plaisir

C'est cet orphelin que tu méprises tel un poison dans les veines
C'est le vol, le viol, la traîtrise pour devise à applaudir

La maîtresse de Dieu
N'a par contre jamais entaché à sa sainteté
Et Dieu même le sais, il est toujours mieux
D'avoir à côté de soi ce qui peut faire échouer

Alors si comme moi
Cela t'énerve et t'offusque
Dis non à cette maîtresse en toi
Car Dieu ne partage pas sa maîtresse sans risque

Hier encore (Enfants de la rue)
Fraubi Amel

Hier encore
Pendant ma petite promenade
J'ai vu malgré mon désaccord
Certains visages tristement malades

Malades d'un manque d'affection
Malades d'un manque d'amour
Malades d'un manque d'habitation
Malades à cause de certains vautours

Combien sont-ils ces petits anges
Âmes innocentes dont les tripes
Chantent en chœur une faim aussi sage
À l'orée de ces jours festifs qui constipent

Combien sont-ils à dormir à la belle étoile
Contemplant dans la peine et dans la haine
Ce jour où l'univers a déchiré le voile
Pour les ramener à la réalité, à cette vie soudaine

Enfin, combien sont-ils à prier chaque soir
Un triste Dieu qui leur accordera la chance
De quitter cette terre où la justice est peinte en noir
Pour la terre du côlon comme une délivrance

Mettez-vous à nouveau sur vos trente-et-un
Pour servir de beaux discours infâmes

À des enfants qui n'ont de télévision qu'un ventre à jeun
Qui même au final se foutent d'un texte de Slam

Je vomis ce système politique africain
Où les enfants pullulent les rues en quémandant
Un regard bienveillant qui ressentira cette faim sans fin
Pendant que le droit des enfants ne nourrit que vos enfants

Hier encore
Pendant ma petite promenade
J'ai vu malgré mon désaccord
Certains visages tristement malades

À toi qui part
Fraubi Amel
Lumière taciturne
Vent frais et glacial
Sentier caduque et morne
Grisaille enchantement fluviale

À chacun de ses pas
Au porte de l'infinie vie
Tu le condamnes à toi
À ces souvenirs qui à jamais, vous lient

Désormais à contre gré
Le temps est suspendu
La mer s'est asséchée
Dans un cœur fendu et fondu

À toi qui part
Aux souvenirs qui restent
Que le temps répare
Sans jamais user en lui tes restes

Souffle ! Souffle ! Souffle !
Encore plus fort sans perdre le nord
Le vent d'Est a fait rafale
Laissant nos corps en vie comme morts
Danse ! Danse ! Danse !
Encore et encore auréole sur la tête
La faucheuse est cette dernière danse

À laquelle chacun de nous s'y prête

Le dernier train pour le dernier voyage
Les derniers sourires pour les dernières larmes
Comme un oiseau qui délaisse sa cage
Comme un au revoir, bon voyage belle âme

À toi qui part
Aux souvenirs qui restent
Que le temps répare
Sans jamais user en lui tes restes

Son de sirène
Kane Nabalemwendé Athanase

Ailleurs, la science renonce aux vacances
Pour que l'humanité avance.
Les tentacules de la mort reculent
Où des hercules de la médecine les acculent.
Tel un oisillon, le progrès à l'embryon décolle
Avec les ailes du zèle et de l'école.
Ailleurs, le labeur ignore les vacances
Pour assurer au monde sa quotidienne pitance.
Là-bas, la faim a enfin une fin
Car la main de l'humain n'attend plus l'obole du destin.
Le parchemin devient une boussole de chemin
Par le refus souverain des modèles suzerains.

Ici le labeur désœuvré est en vacances,
L'oisiveté nage dans les réjouissances.
Et toi, mon frère au garde-à-vous,
Tu contemples ébahi ces gratte-ciel debout !
Ton bras viril qui, hélas !, épouse la paresse
Endort le commun essor comme une ivresse.
Ici l'innovation avorte à la conception
Et l'esprit se fait stérile telle une contraception.
Me démange l'ouïe le discours de l'homme de science
Dont le verbe pèse plus lourd que la compétence.
Çà et là hurlent les sirènes qui appellent au labeur
Et toi, mon frère né de la peine, tu fuis la douleur.
Réveille, ô Sirène, mon beau monde qui dort
Qui dort et, sans cesse, accuse à tort le sort.

Siège

Kane Nabalemwendé Athanase

Comme un cerbère en colère
La terreur rôde enragée à nos frontières.
Les turbans noirs flottent en sinistres étendards
Comme des ombres de la mort sur nos remparts.
La paix apeurée s'est déjà exilée de la cité
Sous les huées des armes et des atrocités.
Voici que se lève l'ouragan de la déportation
Qui emporte les exilés dans leur pérégrination.
La meute des armes qui aboient dans les brousses
Sont des messagers de la mort à nos trousses.
La faim règne dans les ménages au foyer éteint
Où l'hebdomadaire poignée de riz est un festin.

La terreur rode enragée aux portes de ma patrie
Esseulée dans sa douleur telle une veuve meurtrie.
Les garants de paix ont un silence assourdissant
Qui donne le feu vert aux tenants et aboutissants.
L'impérialisme sangsue affûte ses lâches crochets
Depuis les couloirs sanguinolents de lointains palais.
Les secours des amis ont la ponctualité du corbillard
Quand l'aide promise à grands cris arrive en retard.
Les prédateurs du monde ont acté l'embargo d'armes
Qui laisse libre cours à l'effusion de sang et de larmes.
Et devant ce siège, un peuple debout dans la résilience
Un peuple debout proclame haut son indépendance.

Laissés-pour-compte
Kane Nabalemwendé Athanase

L'abondance oisive s'ennuie sur les tables de l'opulence
Où les convives mendient un tout petit peu d'indigence.
L'appétit est un dieu que l'on supplie comme un enfant,
A coups d'apéritifs on affame l'embonpoint bedonnant.
Chez les poches policées qui ont goût à tous les couverts
Les banquets se déclinent en entrée, principal et dessert.
Toute la journée se meuble de goûter et d'amuse-gueule,
Sans repas dans la bouche, la langue oisive s'ennuie seule.
Ainsi l'on donne du repas à son temps, non du temps au repas
Dans l'espoir d'échapper par la bombance à l'alezan du trépas.

L'abondance s'ennuie seule dans le domicile de l'opulence
Tandis que l'indigence contraint des bouches à l'abstinence.
Des bouches affamées sous des yeux qui voient l'insolence
Perdent leur éloquence : l'indigence les contraint au silence.
Les uns mangent des yeux ce que d'autres foulent aux pieds,
L'élan d'amour naturel sur les sentiers du cœur s'est estropié.
Ces crève-la-faim sont le procès de toute insolente opulence
Dont l'indifférence devant l'indigence écœure la conscience.
L'humanisme s'indigne du scandale de ces laissés-pour-compte
Dont le silence éloquent couvre l'opulence d'un manteau de honte.

Le Destin
Mondo Kobi Arnold

L'avoir n'a pas vu croire,
ni le désir n'enfante plaisir
dans tous les coins
et recoins des hypocrites.
Au beau milieu du jour,
l'air ne me fait que chanter
l'orage près du marché d'hommage.
Mais tout ce que le vent me chuchote
n'a rien de tel, ni ceux qui s'acclament
ne proclament pas l'heureux.
Même sous le silence mon histoire
se courtise son comble.
Hélas ! Dorénavant, mon heure est pure
et mes vers sont verts comme la frondaison nouvelle.
Si les animaux, les insectes et les herbes ne savent ni le jour,
ni les circonstances de leur fin, mais se réjouissent et dansent,
Alors pourquoi ne pas profiter de cette existence,
qui n'annonce pas l'éternité ?
vraiment le temps est court,
les lendemains incertains mais la vie est belle.
Baignons nous dans cette chanson d'arôme
et célébrons un avenir nouveau,
tel sera notre destin.

Nouvelle journée
Mondo Kobi Arnold

Une nouvelle journée commence,
Lève-toi, pars à sa rencontre
Lève-toi, pars à sa rencontre
Avec pleine d'allégresse et d'espérance,
Lève-toi, pars à sa rencontre
Lève-toi, pars à sa rencontre
Avec plein de courage et de force,
Lève-toi, pars à sa rencontre
Lève –toi, pars à sa rencontre
Elle t'attend en toute confiance,
Lève-toi, pars à sa rencontre
Lève-toi, pars à sa rencontre
Tout en énergie et en justice,
Lève-toi, va la rejoindre
Lève-toi, va la rejoindre
Elle s'ennuie dans ton silence,
Lève-toi, va la rejoindre
Lève-toi, va la rejoindre
Sinon elle partira à l'insu de ta présence
Lève-toi, va la rejoindre
Lève-toi, va la rejoindre
Elle veut partir avec ta clairvoyance
Lève-toi, va la rejoindre
Lève-toi, va à la rejoindre
Elle part avec ta bienséance
Lève-toi vite, va la rejoindre

Lève-toi vite, va la rejoindre
Cours après elle,
Lève-toi, cours après elle
Elle part avec ton extase
Oui, elle est partie…

Extase
Mondo Kobi Arnold

Mon amour, je t'offre cette
guirlande pleine d'hibiscus,
tel est mon frangipanier
et ma gageure à toi.
Je t'invite à ma demeure,
près d'un atoll pharamineux,
garni d'un lagon où baignera
notre amour, pour ne point
se perdre, ce qui est mon antre.

Mon amour, je te façonne
Ce mappemonde couronné
De plaisir et de charme,
Au goût paradisiaque de ta vise
pour te faire ressentir la dose
de ma passion, au bain d'une profonde
jouissance, et oubliant toute gouffre
d'horreurs vécus, afin de te
procurer une joie extrême.

O, mon amour, je t'ouvre tout mon cœur
Et t'offre tout mon être,
coffre et siège de mes trésors.
Viens, installe ton royaume,
Reine en romance et emporte
moi vers le paroxysme de plaisir

pour ensuite vivre mon extase.

À jamais ma langue ne se vêtira de crainte
Wankpo Franck

Gardez comme le lampion affamé votre bouche close
Et comme le soleil, je répandrai mes rayons
Mes rayons dont rien de ténébreux n'échappent,
Comme le vent loquace et sage, je sifflerai les vermines,
Comme des oiseaux tisserins, je chanterai les gloires.

Gardez-la close comme un essoufflé
Et comme le vent violent, je dévoilerai les sales dessous,
Comme un sage, j'acclamerai les purs et limpides dessous,
Comme le feu, je consumerai d'un passage les fausses pailles,
Comme la voix calme, silencieuse et sage,
Je vous dirai ceci qui pour vous ressemble à une incantation,
Je vous dirai :
Vous vous trahissez comme l'esprit vermineux avant l'exécution de son acte.

Gardez-la bée comme un sans vie
Et comme le feu de chaudronnerie, je vous ferai danser à une barre de fer de cent
Que les secondes rompront et briseront,
Comme une flaque d'eau,
 Vous disparaissez dans une apparence fanée aux goûts des démunies.

Tyran, sadique, dangereux que tu sois,
À jamais ma langue ne se vêtira de crainte

À une épopée seront chantés mes sacrifices
Comme les lundis matins de 72,
Tous feront allégeance à mes lauriers.

Intellectuel
Wankpo Franck
Ton cœur est un grand tambour
Dont les résonnances répondent aux appels aux secours
Sans avoir d'arrières pensés.
Les désespoirs minant tes pensées
Ne doivent guère être traduits par ta soif du bon sens.
Comme un catholique, ta soif de foi est ta soif du bon sens.
Foi égale à bon sens.
La foi ! Est-ce une essence ?
Ou sa conscience à accepter d'être aveugle ?
La foi ! Une complétude ?
Ou une vacuité ?
La foi se serait un couple,
La foi se serait un dada.
Hum ! Hors de tout cela. Et si elle est un Juda !

Bats-toi car l'histoire est une silhouette
Une silhouette qui te suit comme la tienne
Tienne contre qui tu ne saurais lutter.
Lutter ! Ton histoire n'a rien avec l'hilarité
Hilarité ! Ni l'ironie
Ironie ! Ni la parodie
Parodie ! Certes, elle est ta vie, ta gratitude du souffle
Souffle envers l'Ubique
Ubique ! Ta vie est une lutte
Une lutte de libération
Libération ! Une lutte de défense
Défense ! Ta vie est l'humanité

Humanité ! Ta vie est celle des autres.

Ne vis pas la vie des autres
Laisse les autres vivre ta vie, qui est autre ;
Ne parle pas parce qu'il faut parler
Mais parle pour émouvoir, élucider, réveiller, libérer ;
Ne brandis pas le sabre parce que le besoin se fait sentir
Brandis-le pour une bonne raison: convertir.

Ta vie doit être l'étoile pour scintiller le ciel et pénétrer les hommes
Les hommes quand les étoiles seront absentes
Absentes en abandonnant une chaîne de ténèbres
Chaîne de ténèbres émouvante drapée leur cerveau embarrassé
Ployé par la chaleur.

C'est toi, Intellectuel
Le taciturne loquace.

Chair odieuse
Wankpo Franck

Adieu Dieu blanc des Blancs !
Derechef bienvenue mes Dieux !
Regagnez sereinement vos sièges longtemps houleux,
Perdues des crédules incrédules
Qui, à la lueur dansent la danse blanche,
Chantant les chansons blanches
Sur un sentier inconnu menant à une destination inconnue,
Donnent leur dixième quotidien, mensuel voire annuel à un vil chômeur
Vil chômeur se cherchant de la médiation des magies raccompagnées de paroles ;
De paroles déroutantes, insolites, transformatrices, déconcertantes ;
De paroles appauvrissantes des âmes pauvres pour la pauvreté éternelle.
Chaire odieuse !
Ouvres tes prunelles,
Étends tes écoutes,
Regarde autour de toi,
Questionne-toi.
L'âme qui s'héberge dans la parole de vie grandit,
Disent-ils.
Le beau parleur te défend l'idolâtrie
Tous vous vous endimanchez vos croix,
Le vil chômeur te défend de ne Jamais t'agenouiller
Devant un regroupement de sable,
Devant une sculpture, un buste

Alors que mille et mille fois vous vous prosternez
hebdomadairement devant le sanctuaire,
Mille et mille fois vous vous agenouillez pour recevoir les
bénédictions de ce prophète.
Chaire odieuse ! Chaire odieuse ! Science-toi. Repents-toi.

Religieux ou chrétien ?
Dis-toi religieux
Car tu ne suis pas la sainte Trinité,
Combien sont-ils à marcher selon la sainte Trinité ?
Religieux est celui qui se vêt de ses jolis décents et indécents habits
Le jour des cultes pour crier, chanter, chamailler,
Jouer et danser avec toute puissance possible
Afin de se débarrasser un instant de ses misères ;
Religieux est celui-là même qui remet en cause sa chrétienté ;
Religieux est celui qui déjeune à la table de la Trinité et dine avec le
diable.

Diable ! C'est les mauvaises intentions auxquelles l'homme se laisse
dominer
Et Non les dieux, nos dieux, nos cultures, nos identités.
Diable, c'est la barbarie humaine et Non Lègba,
Qui est une divinité, un gardien, une escorte.
Détrompe-toi car il est temps,

Être chrétien n'est pas forcément être membre d'une congrégation
religieuse,
Crier le non de la Trinité toute la journée
Mais suivre le jour comme la nuit la Trinité ;

Suivre les lois que la Trinité à la Nature a empruntées
Ces lois dont nous connaissons Moïse.

La Trinité, c'est la Nature.
Comme la Trinité, la Nature ne juge, ne condamne guère
Accepte le pécheur malgré son aversion aux péchés
L'ensevelit dans son ventre au dernier jour.

Impotentes sem Deus
Maria Menezes

Curvados entre escombros nas trevas do fumo
seguiram os sons de tosse e gemidos.
Gritaram em vão os nomes dos seus,
suplicaram misericórdia aos céus.

Coragem e orlas das camisas sobre as bocas,
os dedos tocando peles viscosas.
Arrastaram os corpos feridos
das sombras para a luz, agradecidos.

Mentes sonolentas e aflitas
com sangues nas mãos que não eram os seus,
despertaram corações disparados
dos pesadelos onde foram caçados!

Não eram eles que sucumbiam ao desespero!
Eram irmãos em Gaza, Ucrânia, Arménia,
Iémen, Síria, Congo, Sudão, Mali…
Paquistão, Azerbaijão, Mianmar, Haiti, …

Se vivem, sobrevivem impotentes sem Deus!
No vazio das lágrimas que secaram,
sem paz, sem liberdade, sem licenças,
estão rostos desesperados com doenças.

Ergue-te
Maria Menezes

Inspira!
Retesa os músculos,
crepite osso, faísque nervo;
Exala o ar, espreguiça-te.
Dos poentes aos crepúsculos
de ti és dono, não servo.
Ergue-te!

Enfrenta a cortina de fumo,
um cruzamento, ou duas portas,
mexe-te!
Decide-te por um rumo,
cospe tradições mortas.
Ergue-te!

Acaso a alma se disfarce monocolor
nao te percas no branco insondável,
levanta-te!
Não penses no horror...
Implode-te apenas no sonho viável.
Ergue-te!

Um menino na praia
Maria Menezes

Rondou-me um menino à beira mar:
- *"Amiga olha... estão a estragar!"*
Disse apontando o mangal na praia de água e sal!
Deambulámos pela areia lodosa,
calcário corroído na concha porosa,
verdes de fungos em conchas divas,
plásticos moles como águas vivas.

Uma bacia espreitava lodacenta,
achatadas garrafas tornadas cinzentas,
vidros, alumínios, chinelas, sapatos,
testemunhos humanos de maus atos.

A bacia de pontas como farpas,
casa nova de caracolitos e lapas,
reforçava a desgraça se o menino dizia
- *Tão feia está a baía!*

- *Não deixem nem enterrem aqui lixos,*
desenterram-nos cães ou outros bichos...
Levem-nos quando saírem da praia -
Pediu ele em nome da Praia.

Inferno
Orlando Mussaengana

O Inferno é o cofre dos encapuzados
E o celeiro dos audazes.
É o brilho de tesouros resguardados
Pelas ossadas dos incapazes.

O Inferno foi inventado
Para aprisionar as curiosidades
E alimentar obesidades das seitas.

É *hallal*, o donativo
Do crente que hostiliza ao povo?

Contra *sensu*
Orlando Mussaengana

O corrupto, que à corrupção combate
Ou é demente
Ou mente tal façanha.

Há cajus nas bananeiras
Como há escravos nas cadeiras dos reis.

As 3 faces da moeda
Orlando Mussaengana

O prazo
O guizo
E o sorriso.

As mãos que capinam
Não sabem que a boca que apedreja
Verga-se ao peso do vento esquivo.

Apenas capinam
E apenas apedreja
Para o deleite efémero de um poder sem povo.

I Quiçá Amor
Jéssica Samara

Se algum dia vivenciar um amor de verdade
Quero que seja você
Quero me aconchegar em veredas de esperança
Repletos de importância

Se algum dia encontrar o amor
Quero que seja notado
Partir para todo canto com espanto

Se algum dia meu amor for seu
Espero que o guarde
Que o proteja como a condensa
Destemida e modesta

Não me deixa afogar em descrença
Nem nos problemas em aparência
Mas...! Se algum dia eu vivenciar um amor
Você será o herdeiro!

II Quiçá Amor
Jéssica Samara

Oxalá seu amor me complete
E seu braço me aperte
Incendiando todo o meu ser

Oxalá seu corpo me aqueça
Ainda mais que a coberta
Com uma paixão intensa

Oxalá esse amor permaneça
De década em década
E os deixe de boca aberta

Oxalá meu amor te complete
Como espelho que reflete
A luz que a si se é entregue

Oh! Tenho cá um lembrete
Daqueles de enfeite
Com corda e pingente
Para um amor inexperiente

Sentimentos ardentes
Sentidos fluentes
E um olhar quente

Oxalá eu seja o suficiente

Para apoiar esse amor
E tudo que dele for feito.

III Quiçá Amor
Jéssica Samara

O amor não tem portas
quem dera as estivesse
o amor não tem hortas
mas é como se tivesse

O amor vem para os que o esperaram e pedem
Mas a dor espera até que o mesmo adormeça

Quem dera soubesse
Quem dera alguém me dissesse
Nada mudaria
Mas também não mataria

Você não foi decepção
Mas quem dera fosse paixão
Não quebrou meu coração
Mas ainda assim eis a questao

Quem dera esteja seguro
Do escuro que me deixou
Hhmmm…. Justo!

Não foi você quem não soube amar
Não foi você que se escondeu sob o mar
Não é você quem tenta se afastar
Mas ainda assim tende se culpar

O amor não tem preço
Mas tem endereço
O amor não é escrito
Mas sim expresso

Quem dera soubesse dantes
Quem dera você me alertasse

Que seu amor é como o som
As zombadas fervendo o sangue
Mas se ausente, somente prantos
Chicoteadas arfantes, um eco falante
E o ego comandante

Culpa sua o não dito
Só por isso
Tenho isto!

Embora nunca mais o veja
Espero que não me esqueça
Nem das parvoíces e mesquíces
Espero que se mantenha com estilo e atenta

Pois se algum dia voltar a amar
Quem dera seja você
Mas se algum dia voltar a amar
Estaria traindo você.

Fragmentos do acaso
Gerson Leonardo Matusse

Fico a olhar o céu de soslaio,
à beira do mar
que separa as superfícies
onde maneamos os espíritos
ora fatigados, ora em excessivo vigor.
O meu corpo tirita, débil,
a forçar a ígnea memória
de um olhar tenaz, quase possessivo.
A minha mente titubia, frígida,
a amar-te, a predizer-te, a desejar-te,
porque aqui outrora te conservaste
indecifrável entre os meus braços.
Agora dói-me que te tenhas ido,
agora ajoelho apenas
que o meu nome vibre
ainda no teu peito,
que ao contemplares o sol
te lembres que se te queimas
é porque penso em ti com fervor.

No céu da minha boca
adejam poemas multicolores,
sempre hesitantes, sempre convulsivos.
E eles asfixiam-me,
por isso grito
a centímetros de um ataúde

o mesmo com a gravura epistolar
da tua despedida.
Epitáfio ou não,
aprendi a medir este líquido abismo
enquanto me brotavam doloridas asas
nas costas e no aviso da evaporação.

A Técnica da Coisa
Gerson Leonardo Matusse

A mais viva reticência
se esconde na incógnita fenomenal,
e antes de morrermos,
temos tempo para gritar às escondidas
provocando paralelas inquietações.
Ora, edifica-se um ser
com os olhos que se estendem
sobre a terra e sobre o mar,
e com as mãos que se prolongam
para acariciar os cabelos dos anjos e das divindades afins.

Servimo-nos, eu e vocês,
do mais alto delírio de grandeza
para, ao espelho, ajustarmos as gravatas
e sentirmo-nos homens,
nós, filhos de África.

A Fénix
Lorna Zita

Eu sou a fénix, que renasce das cinzas,
Do fogo que me consome, eu me recrio.
Queimo tudo que me prende ao passado,
Eu volto, mais forte, mais livre, mais fria.

Eu sou a fénix, a alma que nunca se apaga,
A escuridão não me derrota, ela me guia.
O que antes era dor, hoje se faz canto,
Pois da destruição, nasce a minha melodia.

Amores vêm e vão
Lorna Zita

Amores são como ventos suaves,
que tocam a alma sem avisar,
trazem promessas, mas também lágrimas,
pintando de cores o que há de mais profundo no olhar.

Amores nascem em silêncios,
no espaço entre o querer e o temer,
são marés que vêm e vão,
e nos ensinam a perder e a renascer.

São toques suaves e chamas intensas,
São ecos que ficam no ar,
E no fim, o amor se vai mas deixa a presença.

Amores não são para entender,
mas para sentir sem lamentos.
São labirintos que nos perdem,
Mas que também nos guiam.

Àfrica e o dilema da fé
Jaime Fernando Sigaúque

Sou África, Criatura sem luz!
Ah, Sou África criatura sem luz
presa em rituais demoníacos.
Sou África, carregando a santa cruz,
a marca da besta que me fora imprimido
Sim, Sou Eu! O guardião o desterro,
e sendo sincero, se todo Homem é filho de Deus
é bem provável que eu seja fruto de adultério!
Pois até ontem a terra que me nasceu
não me revelou tais mistérios
Sim, hoje a minha fé compadeceu,
as revelações da terra que me nasceu
não foram nada sério!
É, sou um filho de Deus, sem lei
que cruza os Braços enquanto o amor e a Fé
lhe são revelados ao braço de Ferro!
Ah, Conhecerás a Verdade e ela te libertará?!?
Eu não sei de que verdade se trata,
pois nesse mundo de fantasia
eu nunca me senti preso
Ah, em nome do pai e do filho
a nossa terra mãe fora abençoada,
e temos que doar a décima parte da produção
pois a eterna bênção tem preço
O preço da expiação, que eu inocente mal esqueço

Ohh impuros!
calem os tambores, queimem os amuletos,
as imundas ramelas que vos impedem de ver
Encolham as dores, e repousem no leito
que o sofrimento no mundo é dever!
Ah, escutei a voz do meu humilde frei,
âncora dos que não crêem,
a dita marca da castidade
Ah, quem usa mágica é fora da lei,
requebra o nível da Fé,
ao engolir tal verdade
Ah hoje, hoje sei que existe salvação,
E meio olho aguço na privação,
seguindo como Jó
que acolhe qualquer mal que surge!
Sim, por isso hoje exulto na aflição,
e busco a redenção,
do chicote sem nenhum dó,
me esforço a carregar a cruz

Cobra Versus Maria Café
Jaime Fernando Sigaúque

Maria café, tão preta ela é, é castanha também
A Maria café nasceu com mil pés,
dádiva da natureza que não lhe levou tão além
Sim, a Maria café tem um escudo de calcário,
e se move em linha como um forte trem,
mas é vista a descarrilar aos pinos,
com cheiro de qualquer sapatear quem vem
Sim, a Maria café tem mil compartimentos,
que se desfazem facilmente, frágeis,
um pouco de pressão, que as entranhas ardem!
A serpente é um plástico de ver,
fricção sobre ele no calor da emoção,
todas as florestas ardem!
Sim a serpente, é uma borracha ao ver
mas suporta a pressão com coragem,
ela se alonga se encolhe, em suspeitas viagens
A maria café, se pisa e morre, não tem força para se levantar,
pisa a serpente, tão mole, invicta, não cai!
A Maria café se acha fértil em ambientes húmidos,
até que as águas ataquem!
Aí ela procura refúgio,
alguma cabana até que as folhas a abracem
Olha a serpente, uma dádiva do ambiente,
corre na água, aspira o pó do deserto,

um exemplo para os impotentes

A Maria café alimenta-se de restos de frutos,
vegetais em decomposição,
ajuda a recomposição dos solos,
reclamada pelos herbívoros!
A serpente escala as árvores, mas não
para sugar os seus frutos,
mas para sugar o sangue, das aves de colo,
foi assim que encarnou a agilidade de alguns mamíferos
Sim, a serpente herdou o saltar das Rãs,
o correr dos ratos, um reforço para o seu íntimo
A serpente silencia o veneno do anfíbio mudo,
se reconcilia com o gambá,
que não aceita baixar o escudo!
As fábulas da nossa mãe África!
A serpente invade todos buracos profundos
Presa que late, que tenha um fundo no esgoto.

Piratas das caraíbas
Jaime Fernando Sigaúque

Piratas das Caraíbas mirando as nossas ilhas.
Piratas das Caraíbas mirando as nossas ilhas,
um simples balão de terra, pesado para as nossas filhas
Piratas da Caraíbas, farejando qualquer fundo que brilha,
com intuito de passar a perna, onde a nossa mão não trilha
Piratas da Caraíbas, tentando infestar algumas milhas!
Onde semeiam brotos eternos, como fizeram nas Antilhas
Piratas das Caraíbas, que me arrastaram pela corrente
como um iceberg que paira sem nenhum chão!
vagando neste mar ardente, com risco de dissolver noutra nação
Piratas das Caraíbas, a mão que fora ungida
para baptizar-me nas margens do Saint Martin
Ah Piratas das Caraíbas, que tomaram a minha alma caída,
que invocava o espírito do Benjamin Franklin.

Mmap New African Poets Series

If you have enjoyed *Best New African Poets 2025 Anthology*, consider these other fine books in the **Mmap New African Poets Series** from *Mwanaka Media and Publishing*:

I Threw a Star in a Wine Glass by Fethi Sassi
Best New African Poets 2017 Anthology by Tendai R Mwanaka and Daniel Da Purificacao
Logbook Written by a Drifter by Tendai Rinos Mwanaka
Mad Bob Republic: Bloodlines, Bile and a Crying Child by Tendai Rinos Mwanaka
Zimbolicious Poetry Vol 1 by Tendai R Mwanaka and Edward Dzonze
Zimbolicious Poetry Vol 2 by Tendai R Mwanaka and Edward Dzonze
Zimbolicious: An Anthology of Zimbabwean Literature and Arts, Vol 3 by Tendai Mwanaka
Under The Steel Yoke by Jabulani Mzinyathi
Fly in a Beehive by Thato Tshukudu
Bounding for Light by Richard Mbuthia
Sentiments by Jackson Matimba
Best New African Poets 2018 Anthology by Tendai R Mwanaka and Nsah Mala
Words That Matter by Gerry Sikazwe
The Ungendered by Delia Watterson
Ghetto Symphony by Mandla Mavolwane
Sky for a Foreign Bird by Fethi Sassi
A Portrait of Defiance by Tendai Rinos Mwanaka
Zimbolicious: An Anthology of Zimbabwean Literature and Arts, Vol 4 by Tendai Mwanaka and Jabulani Mzinyathi

When Escape Becomes the only Lover by Tendai R Mwanaka
وِيَسْ مَرُ اللّيْلُ فِىَ ثِفَتَنِي...وَلْ عَمَام by Fethi Sassi
A Letter to the President by Mbizo Chirasha
This is not a poem by Richard Inya
Pressed flowers by John Eppel
Righteous Indignation by Jabulani Mzinyathi:
Blooming Cactus by Mikateko Mbambo
Rhythm of Life by Olivia Ngozi Osouha
Travellers Gather Dust and Lust by Gabriel Awuah Mainoo
Chitungwiza Mushamukuru: An Anthology from Zimbabwe's Biggest Ghetto Town by Tendai Rinos Mwanaka
Zimbolicious: An Anthology of Zimbabwean Literature and Arts, Vol 5 by Tendai Mwanaka
Because Sadness is Beautiful? by Tanaka Chidora
Of Fresh Bloom and Smoke by Abigail George
Shades of Black by Edward Dzonze
Best New African Poets 2020 Anthology by Tendai Rinos Mwanaka, Lorna Telma Zita and Balddine Moussa
This Body is an Empty Vessel by Beaton Galafa
Between Places by Tendai Rinos Mwanaka
Best New African Poets 2021 Anthology by Tendai Rinos Mwanaka, Lorna Telma Zita and Balddine Moussa
Zimbolicious: An Anthology of Zimbabwean Literature and Arts, Vol 6 by Tendai Mwanaka and Chenjerai Mhondera
A Matter of Inclusion by Chad Norman
Keeping the Sun Secret by Mariel Awendit
سِجِلٌّ مَكْتُوبٌ لِتَغَاه by Tendai Rinos Mwanaka
Ghetto Blues by Tendai Rinos Mwanaka

Zimbolicious: An Anthology of Zimbabwean Literature and Arts, Vol 7 by Tendai Rinos Mwanaka and Tanaka Chidora
Best New African Poets 2022 Anthology by Tendai Rinos Mwanaka and Helder Simbad
Dark Lines of History by Sithembele Isaac Xhegwana
a sky is falling by Nica Cornell
Death of a Statue by Samuel Chuma
Along the way by Jabulani Mzinyathi
Strides of Hope by Tawanda Chigavazira
Young Galaxies by Abigail George
Coming of Age by Gift Sakirai
Mother's Kitchen and Other Places by Antreka. M. Tladi
Best New African Poets 2023 Anthology by Tendai Rinos Mwanaka, Helder Simbad and Gerald Mpesse
Zimbolicious Anthology Vol 8 by Tendai Rinos Mwanaka and Mathew T Chikono
Broken Maps by Riak Marial Riak
Formless by Raïs Neza Boneza
Of poets, gods, ghosts. Irritants and storytellers by Tendai Rinos Mwanaka
Ethiopian Aliens by Cleisidia Nzorozwa
In The Inferno by Jabulani Mzinyathi
Who Told You To Be God by Mariel Awendit
Nobody Loves Me by Abigail
The Stories of Stories by Nkwazi Mhango
Nhorido by Siphosami Ndlovu and Tinashe Chikumbo
Best New African Poets 10th Anniversary: Selected English African Poets by Tendai Rinos Mwanaka
Best New African Poets 10th Anniversary: Interviews and Reviews of African Poets by Tendai Rinos Mwanaka

Best New African Poets 10th Anniversary: African Languages and Collaborations by   Tendai Rinos Mwanaka
ANTOLOGIA DOS MELHORES "NOVOS" POETAS AFRICANOS 10º Aniversário: Poetas Africanos Da Língua Portuguesa Selecionados by Lorna Telma Zita and Tendai Rinos Mwanaka
ABRACADABRA, by Olivia Ngozi Osuoha
DES MEILLEURS "NOUVEAUX" POÈTES AFRICAINS 10ᵉ Anniversaire : Poètes africains d'expression française by Geraldin Mpesse and Tendai Rinos Mwanaka
Taurai Amai by Cosmas Tasvika Manhanhanha
Nhemeramutupo by Oscar Gwiriri
Ntombentle: Selected Poems by Sithembele Isaac Xhegwana
African Poetry Anthology: Chapbooks, Vol 1 by Tendai Rinos Mwanaka, Lorna Telma Zita and Helder Simbad
Juices Of The Forbidden Fruit by Tapuwa Tremor, Mapaike
Like The Starry Night Sky, by Obinna Chilekezi
The Stench by Jabulani Mzinyathi
African Languages Poetry Anthology Vol 1 by Tendai Rinos Mwanaka
The Tear of an Ophan Child by Mwanaka Fombe